HISTORY OF IDEAS IN ANCIENT GREECE

This is a volume in the Arno Press collection

HISTORY OF IDEAS IN ANCIENT GREECE

Advisory Editor
Gregory Vlastos

See last pages of this volume for a complete list of titles

PLATO'S LAW OF SLAVERY

IN ITS RELATION TO GREEK LAW

BY

GLENN R. MORROW

ARNO PRESS

A New York Times Company

New York / 1976

Editorial Supervision: EVE NELSON

Reprint Edition 1976 by Arno Press Inc.

Reprinted from a copy in
The University of Illinois Library

HISTORY OF IDEAS IN ANCIENT GREECE
ISBN for complete set: 0-405-07285-6
See last pages of this volume for titles.

Manufactured in the United States of America

Library of Congress Cataloging in Publication Data

Morrow, Glenn Raymond, 1895-
Plato's law of slavery in its relation to Greek law.

(History of ideas in ancient Greece)
Reprint of the 1939 ed. published by the University of Illinois Press, Urbana, which was issued as v. 25, no. 3, of Illinois studies in language and literature.
1. Plato. Leges. 2. Slavery in Greece. 3. Law, Greek. I. Title. II. Series. III. Series: Illinois. University. Illinois studies in language and literature ; v. 25, no. 3.
Law 342'.38'087 75-13283
ISBN 0-405-07325-9

ILLINOIS STUDIES IN LANGUAGE AND LITERATURE

VOL. XXV

NO. 3

PUBLISHED BY THE UNIVERSITY OF ILLINOIS
UNDER THE AUSPICES OF THE GRADUATE SCHOOL
URBANA, ILLINOIS

PLATO'S LAW OF SLAVERY

IN ITS RELATION TO GREEK LAW

BY

Glenn R. Morrow

THE UNIVERSITY OF ILLINOIS PRESS

URBANA

1939

To

William Alexander Hammond

in affectionate memory

ACKNOWLEDGMENTS

It is a pleasure to record my gratitude to the many persons who have assisted me in the preparation of this study: to Professor George H. Sabine, of Cornell University, who first suggested to me the idea of exploring the relation between Plato's *Laws* and the legal institutions of the Greeks; to Professor W. A. Oldfather, of the University of Illinois, who read this work in manuscript and gave me searching criticism as well as generous encouragement; to the Universities of Munich and Vienna, for the privileges extended me during the academic year 1933–1934 while I was collecting material, and especially to Professors Albert Rehm, Adolf Wilhelm, and Heinrich Gomperz, for their kindly interest and valuable suggestions; to the Library of the University of Illinois, without the rich resources of which it would have been difficult to proceed, and to its librarians for their part in making these resources available; to Dr. Lloyd W. Daly, of the University of Oklahoma, for assistance in proofreading; and lastly, to my wife, who has assisted me, directly and indirectly, at all stages of the undertaking.

Some paragraphs of the following work, chiefly in the introduction and the concluding chapter, have appeared previously in *Mind* (April, 1939). The editor has generously given permission to reprint this material here.

G. R. M.

CONTENTS

LIST OF ABBREVIATIONS

Apelt	Apelt, Otto, *Platons Gesetze.* 2 vols. Leipzig, 1916.
Archiv	*Archiv für Papyrusforschung.*
Beauchet	Beauchet, Ludovic, *Histoire du Droit Privé de la République Athénienne.* 4 vols. Paris, 1897.
Bonner and Smith	Bonner, Robert J., and Smith, Gertrude, *The Administration of Justice from Homer to Aristotle.* Chicago, Vol. I, 1930; Vol. II, 1938.
Bücheler-Zitelmann	Bücheler, Franz, and Zitelmann, Ernst, *Das Recht von Gortyn.* Frankfurt, 1885.
Busolt	Busolt, Georg, and Swoboda, Heinrich, *Griechische Staatskunde.* Munich, Vol. I, 1920; Vol. II, 1926.
CIA	*Corpus Inscriptionum Atticarum.* Berlin, 1873–1897.
CIG	*Corpus Inscriptionum Graecarum.* Berlin, 1828–1877.
Dikaiomata	[Graeca Halensis], *Dikaiomata: Auszüge aus Alexandrinischen Gesetzen und Verordnungen in einem Papyrus des Philologischen Seminars der Universität Halle* (Pap. Hal. 1). Berlin, 1913.
England	England, E. B., *The Laws of Plato.* 2 vols. Manchester and London, 1921.
IJG	Dareste, Haussoulier, and Reinach, *Recueil des Inscriptions Juridiques Grècques.* Paris, 1891–1904.
Kahrstedt	Kahrstedt, Ulrich, *Staatsgebiet und Staatsangehörige in Athen.* Stuttgart-Berlin, 1934.
Kohler-Ziebarth	Kohler, Josef, and Ziebarth, Erich, *Das Stadtrecht von Gortyn.* Göttingen, 1912.
Lipsius	Lipsius, H. J., *Das Attische Recht und Rechtsverfahren.* Leipzig, 1905, 1908.
Meyer	Meyer, Paul M., *Juristische Papyri.* Berlin, 1920.
OG	Dittenberger, W., *Orientis Graeci Inscriptiones Selectae.* Leipzig, 1903, 1905.
Ritter	Ritter, Constantin, *Platons Gesetze: Darstellung des Inhalts und Kommentar.* 2 vols. 1896.
Sylloge	Dittenberger, W., *Sylloge Inscriptionum Graecarum.* 3rd ed., 2 vols., Leipzig, 1915, 1917. All references are to this edition unless otherwise specified.
Westermann	Westerman, W. L., article "*Sklaverei*" in Pauly-Wissowa, *Realenzyklopädie der Klassischen Altertumswissenschaft.* Supplementband VI, 1935.
ZSS	*Zeitschrift der Savigny-Stiftung.*

INTRODUCTION

The presence of slavery in the *Laws* has puzzled and distressed many of Plato's admirers. Some have interpreted it as a concession to customs of his age to which he was at heart opposed. Others have pointed out various humane aspects of his law of slavery and inferred that even if he did not secretly condemn the institution he at least endeavored to lighten its burdens. Still others have passed over the subject as something from which our gaze should be averted as quickly as possible. But before we can condemn, or excuse, or even properly understand Plato's attitude toward slavery we must first have a clear idea of the legal status of the slave under Plato's law, and compare it with the slave's position under the Greek law of Plato's day. Even a cursory examination shows that Plato's law of slavery, like the other parts of his legislation, is laid down with considerable legal precision; and the number of passages in the *Laws* that deal with slavery is surprisingly large, considering the humble position that slaves occupy in the state. So the systematic examination and exposition of Plato's law of slavery would seem to be both feasible and desirable, though such a task, so far as I know, has never before been undertaken.[1]

Besides throwing light upon its author's attitude toward this "peculiar institution," Plato's law of slavery may well contribute much to our understanding of Greek law. It is one of the most ironical mischances of history that the ancient people who first thought systematically about law in nature and in human conduct should have had so little of their actual legislation preserved. Of the work of the great legislators whose names were revered by all later Greeks —Zaleucus of Locri, Charondas of Catana, Pheidon of Corinth, Draco and Solon of Athens, 'Lycurgus' of Sparta—nothing remains except fragments scattered through the voluminous literature of antiquity, the inscriptions and the papyri. The material is in such an unpromising form that the task of reconstruction was for a long time neglected and the very existence of such a thing as Greek law ignored, if not even denied. But the absurdity of neglecting that aspect

[1] Most students of the *Laws* have called attention to features of Plato's slave law and often have made penetrating comments; e.g. Ritter, in his commentary on the *Laws;* Jowett, in the Introduction to his translation; Chase, in *Harvard Studies in Classical Philology*, Vol. XLIV (1933); England, in the notes to his edition of the Greek text; Apelt, in the notes to his translation. But these comments have been at best fragmentary and sometimes misleading because of the absence of the juristic and historical background upon which alone the details can be understood.

of the Greek genius of which the Greeks themselves were especially proud could not persist forever, and the task of recreating Greek law from the fragments has within the last century attracted a steadily increasing number of workers. The discovery of the great inscription at Gortyn in 1884, together with other fragments of the legislation of Gortyn, gave a tremendous impetus to this enterprise by affording an unobstructed view of a large section of the actual laws in force in a fourth-century Cretan city. Since then the industrious collection and comparison of inscriptions, and the discovery of stores of Egyptian papyri, have put at our disposal much new legal material, of diverse origin in place and time, but by virtue of its very diversity opening up new perspectives and promising a broader basis for systematization than would have been deemed possible a half-century ago. We face the clear prospect of being able to understand Greek law, not indeed with the fullness and clarity with which Roman law has long been known, but with enough accuracy to be able to discern its characteristic principles and procedures, and something of the way in which they developed in the individual Greek cities.[2]

Among the literary sources of Greek law, the *Laws* of Plato occupies a unique place. It is a thorough, systematic, and detailed account of the legislation of an ideal fourth-century Greek city, accompanied by a commentary and discussion of principles. This is the sort of thing which, if it had been done for Athens or Corinth or Syracuse by some ancient observer, would be regarded as a priceless historical document. The fact that Plato did it for a city that existed only in his own imagination, and still more, perhaps, the fact that it was done by a philosopher interested (as the *Republic* shows) in a radical reform of existing institutions, may lead us to doubt whether it can be accepted as a guide to historical realities. But we must remember that the professed purpose of the *Laws* is to draw the outlines of a realizable, albeit second-best state; and such a task requires that the author stick rather closely to the realities of his time. Furthermore, we know that in the years after the writing of the *Republic* Plato had been much occupied with the practical problems of Greek politics. The Academy was founded, in part at least, to serve as a training-school for statesmen, and many of its members actually went out as legislators or legislative consultants to the Greek cities of their day. Plato himself went to Syracuse and tried to reform its

[2] "Offenbar ist eine neue Disziplin im Entstehen," wrote Wilamowitz in 1910 (*Staat und Gesellschaft der Griechen*, p. 207).

government by working through the impressionable young tyrant Dionysius. Along with these ventures into practical politics there seems to have taken place a change of a profounder sort in Plato's philosophical views, a change that led him to value more highly the empirically given materials of history and politics.[3] Considering these contacts between the Academy and the political movements of the fourth century, and this more empirical attitude of Plato's later philosophy, we can be sure that the studies in the Academy were not confined to the delineation of Utopias, but dealt with the realities of fourth-century political life. No one has ever doubted Aristotle's value as a witness to his time. There can be no question that the foundations of Aristotle's mastery of the empirical details of Greek law and politics were laid during the years when he was a pupil in the Academy (years which coincided with the period of Plato's labors on the *Laws*) and that much of this mastery he owed to Plato.[4]

A special aspect of the more empirical approach of Plato's later years is his changed attitude toward the place and function of law. Whereas the guardians of the *Republic* are to exercise power without legal limitations, the sovereignty of law is the key-note of Plato's later political thought. This change of key is evident in the *Politicus*, which affirms that as the world now goes the only legitimate rulers are those who rule in accordance with a law more authoritative than their own will and wisdom. The sovereignty of law is emphatically and eloquently asserted in the *Seventh* and *Eighth Epistles* and is the very basis of the political structure of the *Laws*. (It was this doctrine, not the rule of the philosophers as expressed in the *Republic*, that formed the heart of Plato's teaching at Syracuse).[5] Consequently the disdain expressed in the *Republic*[6] for the details of legislation is replaced in the *Laws* by a pronounced interest in legal formulas and a concern, often meticulous, for niceties of detail. Even one who is disposed on general grounds to find a large measure of juristic matter in the *Laws* may well be amazed at the extent to which Plato's law incorporates details of procedure and technicalities of diction from positive law. But after all, Plato's later attitude toward law is the orthodox Greek attitude, and it should not surprise us that he, or any other educated Greek, should show a famil-

---

[3] See Sabine, *History of Political Theory*, chap. iv.

[4] For the debt of the *Politics* to the *Laws*, see Barker, *Greek Political Theory, Plato and His Predecessors*, pp. 380–382.

[5] See the author's *Studies in the Platonic Epistles*, pp. 139 ff.

[6] IV, 425–426.

iarity with the principles by which the citizens of the *polis* regulated their relations to one another. The sharp distinction that now exists between law and morality, and the parallel distinction between lawyers and ordinary citizens, would probably have seemed strange to a Greek of the fifth century. The citizen had to be his own lawyer, for he might be required to defend himself any day in the courts. He was eligible to sit as a dicast in the city's courts, where his duty was to pass upon the law as well as the facts. He could sit in the Assembly where, if law was not exactly made in the modern sense, it was always being interpreted and frequently being set aside. Knowledge of the law was presumed to be a part of the equipment of the citizen; and if the Greek of the fourth century found it more difficult to acquire this knowledge than it had been for his grandfather, he was not yet ready to relinquish the ideal which the older tradition represented. Plato, it is worth noting, makes the study of the laws a fundamental part of the program of education in the *Laws*.[7]

The value of the *Laws* as a source of information regarding Greek law has often been asserted in vigorous terms. Mitteis called this work "the mirror of Greek law,"[8] and Keil pronounced it superior even to Aristotle's *Politics* as a guide to the spirit and details of the Greek legal mind.[9] Wilamowitz said we must dig in the *Laws* first if we would get at the roots of Greek legal thought and feeling.[10] But the systematic exploration of the *Laws* from the juristic point of view is still in its early stages. A promising beginning was made more than a century ago by Karl Friedrich Hermann in two small studies which for a long time had no successors.[11] Since the beginning of this century several serious studies have been made of special portions of Platonic law. Besides the comprehensive (but less detailed) inquiries

[7] VII, 811d ff. [8] *Reichsrecht und Volksrecht*, p. 237.

[9] *Griechische Staatsaltertümer*, in Gercke and Norden's *Einleitung in die Altertumswissenschaft*, 2nd. ed., p. 382.

[10] *Staat und Gesellschaft*, p. 207. Wilamowitz prefaces this statement with a most interesting account of a conversation with Mommsen. "In the year 1873 I was travelling at night with Mommsen over the plain of Apulia toward Venusia. The first volume of his *Staatsrecht* had just appeared, and I spoke to him with youthful enthusiasm of the impression the book had made upon me and how I was thinking of doing something similar for the Greeks. And I ventured to express the opinion that my inquiry would differ from his chiefly in that for the Greeks one must above all read the philosophers, especially Plato's *Laws*. 'Yes indeed,' he replied eagerly and with full understanding. 'I should have read Plato too. It is perhaps too late for me now, and for that reason I can say very little about your Greeks'."

[11] *Disputatio de vestigiis institutorum veterum imprimis Atticorum per Platonis de Legibus libros indagandis; Juris domestici et familiaris apud Platonem in Legibus cum veteris Graeciae inque primis Athenarum institutis comparatio.* Marburg, 1836.

of Schulte[12] and Chase,[13] Plato's testamentary law has been studied by Bruck,[14] the homicide law by Goetz,[15] the law of the family by Becker,[16] and the economic regulations of Plato's state by Bisinger[17] and Lauffer.[18] These studies have clearly shown that Plato's laws are not merely Platonic, but Greek, both in spirit and in detail; and their success shows the desirability of pushing the inquiry into other special provinces of Plato's legislation.

It has sometimes been claimed that Plato's work was a powerful factor in the shaping of legal institutions in the Hellenistic and Roman periods. Burnet declared that the *Laws* was the "foundation of Hellenistic law," and thus came to exert a powerful influence upon Roman law.[19] The first part of this statement can hardly be taken literally, for the foundation of Hellenistic law is the Greek law of the classical period; but it may still be true that Plato's book had much influence in modifying the classical Greek law. The evidence for such influence is as yet, however, almost totally lacking.[20] The question is one which has been singularly neglected by students of the Platonic tradition, and its examination is the more in order just now in that the related question of the influence of Hellenistic law upon Roman law is attracting the attention of historians and students of comparative law. I have referred but rarely to Roman law and have never, I trust, used it as the basis for an inference as to the principle valid in Greek law. There is manifestly a danger in interpreting Greek practices in the light of Roman principles. The early students of Greek law, most of whom were continental scholars, were inclined

---

[12] Schulte, J., *Quomodo Plato in Legibus publica Atheniensium instituta respexerit.* Diss. Münster, 1907.

[13] Chase, A. H., "The Influence of Athenian Institutions upon the Laws of Plato," *Harvard Studies in Classical Philology*, XLIV (1933), 133–192.

[14] Bruck, E. F., "Die Entstehung des Griechischen Testaments und Platos Nomoi," in *ZSS*, Rom. Abt. XXXII (1911), 353–359. Cf. also Becker, W. G., *Platons Gesetze und das Griechische Erbrecht*, Ohlau i. Schl., 1930.

[15] Goetz, W., *Legum Platonis de Jure Capitali Praecepta cum Jure Attico Comparantur*, Darmstadt, 1912.

[16] Becker, W. G., *Platons Gesetze und das Griechische Familienrecht*, München, 1932.

[17] Bisinger, J., "Der Agrarstaat in Platons Gesetzen," in *Klio*, Beiheft XVII (1925).

[18] Lauffer, S., "Die Platonische Agrarwirtschaft," in *Vierteljahrschrift für Sozial- und Wirtschaftsgeschichte*, XXIX (1936), 233–269.

[19] *Greek Philosophy*, p. 304; see also Barker, *op. cit.* pp. 307, 353. Is there such an implication in Mommsen's remark to Wilamowitz, quoted above (note 10)?

[20] Curiously enough the sole evidence that Burnet cites in support of his statement is evidence of the kind of influence which he says was less important, viz. the direct influence of Plato upon Roman jurists. For Burnet the more important fact is the indirect influence of Plato through Hellenistic law.

to approach it with the conceptual tools of the familiar Roman law. But of late a more cautious attitude has come to prevail. Enough is now known of Greek law to enable us to see that is has a character of its own and on certain points diverges sharply from Roman law.[21] It may be true that the two systems are fundamentally alike, either because they are both products of the legal sense of two peoples who were after all akin, or because Roman law was influenced in its development by the more precocious Greek law. But neither of these points can be clearly established unless we refrain from assuming them in our premises.

In the treatment of the many special problems that follow, I have endeavored first to elicit the principles underlying Plato's legislation on the point under examination, and to elicit them from Plato's text itself, appealing as little as possible to the evidence of positive law until Plato's principles were already clear. Sometimes this was not possible. Some curious detail of his law, some turn of phrase, could not be understood save in the light of principles and institutions not evident in the *Laws* itself. Because of the similarity between Plato's and Aristotle's political views—a similarity that becomes more striking the more one compares the *Laws* and the *Politics*—I have not hesitated on occasion to draw upon Aristotle for clues as to Plato's intentions. After the principles of Platonic law are laid bare, comes the nice task of comparison with positive law. The fragmentary and unsystematic character of the evidence upon which in the main we have to rely for a knowledge of Greek law makes the path of the interpreter no easy one. Here a reference in Antiphon to some "ancestral law" of the Athenians; here an inscription from Asia Minor giving the police regulations in second-century Pergamum; here a papyrus from third-century Alexandria; here a definition or statement of principle by the grammarians, referring presumably to Attic law—such are the sources with which one has to work. To use properly materials of such diverse provenance and content requires the utmost caution. I can only hope that I have generally avoided what Professor Shorey called the besetting vice of the philologist, viz. making the evidence prove more than it legitimately can.

[21] Vinogradoff, P., *Historical Jurisprudence*, II, 7; Wenger, L., *Recht der Griechen und Römer*, *passim*. We shall find, for example, that with respect to slavery there are marked differences between Greek and Roman law.

Chapter I

GENERAL CHARACTERISTICS OF THE SLAVE CLASS

There is nowhere in the *Laws* a systematic account of the slave[1] population, its size, its economic functions, the sources from which it is to be recruited, and the particular form of servitude to which it is to be subjected. Our information on all these points has to be derived from incidental and scattered references and by inference from other institutions of the *Laws*.

From one of these incidental references we learn that there are to be slaves owned by the state (*οἱ τῆς πόλεως οἰκέται*, VII, 794b) as well as privately owned slaves. This reference to the "slaves of the city" would have been easily understood by an Athenian reader, at least, for the use of publicly owned slaves as functionaries of the state was a familiar feature of Athenian life.[2] But very little is said about the functions of such slaves in Plato's state. The above reference to public slaves shows them disciplining children in the schools, under the direction of the supervising matron. Probably they were also used by the magistrates generally, as at Athens, in maintaining public order and in punishing offenders (cf. IX, 882b), and perhaps also in repairing streets and water works in the city (VI, 763 cd). But the distinction between public and private slaves nowhere appears in the slave legislation, and this suggests that the number of the former was not intended to be very great. It is for privately owned slaves, as we shall see, that Plato's legislation is designed.

Of privately owned slaves some belong to citizens and some to

---

[1] The terms most commonly used in the *Laws* to denote slave are *δοῦλος* and *οἰκέτης*. These often seem to be employed interchangeably, as in VI, 763a, 776bc, 777d; VII, 807e, 808a; VIII, 846d, 849c, 853d. The criminal law, however, regularly employs *δοῦλος* (IX, 865c 868a, 872a–c, 881c, 882b; XI, 914a, 914e, 930d, 936c). On a possible distinction between these terms, see Appendix A. Other terms used are *ἀνδράποδον* (XI, 916a), *ἀκόλουθος* (VIII, 845a), *θεράπων* (I, 633c), and *θεραπαινίς* (VII, 808a). All these terms except the last occur frequently in the other Platonic dialogues, in Attic prose, and in the inscriptions (Kretschmer, in *Glotta*, XVIII, 71–81). It is significant that such terms as *πελάτης*, *θής*, and *περίοικοι*, expressive of serfdom, though occurring elsewhere in Plato's dialogues, do not appear in the *Laws*.

[2] A force of Scythian bowmen (*Σκύθαι* or *τοξόται*) was employed to keep order in the streets, market-places, and public assemblies during the fifth century (Schol. to Aristoph. *Acharn.* 54; *Thesmoph.* 940, 1002 ff.; *Lysistr.* 441). Slaves were also used for clerical work in public offices in the fourth century (Dem. VIII, 47; XXII, 70); for building and repairing the streets and public edifices (Arist. *Const. of Athens* LIV, 1) and in other tasks (Arist. *op. cit.* LXV, 4; L, 2); and as executioners (Pollux VIII, 71). See Busolt, pp. 979 ff.; Jacob, O., "Les esclaves publics à Athènes," *Le Musée Belge*, XXX (1926), 57–106. For the use of public slaves in other Greek cities see Westermann, in Pauly-Wissowa, Suppl. VI, 908.

the resident or transient foreigners. The distinction between the slaves of citizens and the slaves of foreigners was apparently of no importance in positive Greek law, but it appears in Plato's legislation because of the distinction he draws between the occupations suitable for citizens and those that are to be left for foreigners. The citizen in Plato's state is to gain his livelihood from the soil and is forbidden to engage in trade or handicraft or in money-lending. Such activities are to be carried on exclusively by the foreigners, either the *metics* or the transient traders admitted for a limited period to the city (VIII, 846d, 849c; cf. XI, 920a; XII, 952e ff.).[3] The basis of this law was the belief, common to Plato and Aristotle, that such vocations are inconsistent with the development of the highest virtue.[4] What is significant for our purpose is that Plato applies his prohibition not merely to citizens but to the slaves of citizens, believing evidently that if the citizen is to be protected from the corrupting effects of industry and trade he must be prohibited from employing his slaves in them. A significant consequence follows. We know that at Athens (and probably elsewhere) in the fourth century there existed a class of slaves who were relatively independent of their masters. They lived apart and conducted enterprises of their own apparently without the supervision of their masters, being obligated to deliver regularly a fixed amount or a certain share of their earnings.[5] It is hard to imagine that even Plato would consider the masters of such slaves in danger of corruption, and the inference is that such a privileged class of slaves is not to exist in Plato's state. In other words, the slave is normally under the direct supervision of his master; he lives in his household and assists him in the occupations, public or private, in which the citizen may engage.

The citizen's slaves will therefore be employed in agricultural labors on his master's land (such as tilling the soil, tending cattle and sheep, VII, 805e, 806d), in domestic tasks about the house (cf. VII, 808ab), or in personal attendance upon his master and his master's children (VII, 808e). When not needed by their masters they may also be employed on public works, such as the building of fortifications, highways, canals, dams, and aqueducts (VI, 760e ff., 763a). Mention is made of slave actors, who perform comic parts be-

[3] Foreigners in turn are excluded from agriculture, except as hired laborers on the citizens' holdings; for the ownership of land is an exclusive prerogative of citizenship.

[4] VII, 807c ff.; Arist. *Pol.* 1277b 33 ff., 1328b 39.

[5] On these δοῦλοι μισθοφοροῦντες see Beauchet, II, 445 ff.; Bekker, *Anecdota*, I, 316, 11; Harpocration, Suidas, and Photius *s.v.* χωρὶς οἰκοῦντες.

neath the dignity of citizens (VII, 816e), and we read also of slave physicians to attend upon sick slaves (IV, 720a ff.; IX, 857cd); but whether these are slaves of the state, slaves of citizens, or slaves of foreigners is not clear.

What is the status of the agricultural slave in Plato's state? In many Greek states—in Lacedaemonia, Argos, Thessaly, Crete, Boeotia, and even in Attica before Solon's time—a form of servitude existed analogous to the serfdom of medieval Europe; and this class of persons was sharply distinguished in law from domestic and industrial slaves.[6] The Helots in Lacedaemonia, for example, were bound to the soil, i.e. they could not change their residence within the country, nor emigrate, nor be sold beyond it; but they were relatively free to carry on the cultivation of their lands as they pleased, subject to the payment of a fixed annual rental to their masters.[7] A passage in the *Laws* has suggested to some interpreters that Plato had in mind a similar arrangement.[8] "The cultivation of the fields is committed to slaves," says this passage, "who deliver to their masters the first-fruits of their labors, an amount sufficient for men who live temperately."[9] Taken alone, this passage might well suggest that the agricultural slaves in Plato's state have a status analogous to that of the Spartan Helots; but when other features and provisions of the *Laws* are examined this conclusion would seem to be unwarranted. In the first place, the passage above quoted must be read in connection with the law governing the distribution of the annual produce (VIII, 847e–848c), which provides that the whole shall be divided into three portions, one part for the citizens (here called freemen),

---

[6] Pollux (III, 83) says there was a class of persons *μεταξὺ ἐλευθέρων καὶ δούλων* and gives as examples the Helots of Lacedaemonia, the Penestae of Thessaly, the Cretan *κλαρῶται* and *μνωῖται*, the *δωροφόροι* of Mariandyni, the *γυμνῆτες* of Argos, and the *κορυνηφόροι* of Sicyon. On serfdom in Boeotia, see Ephorus' Fr. 21(Jacoby). There are evidences of serfdom also at Byzantium and in Locris. See Wallon, *Histoire de l'esclavage dans l'antiquité*, I, 133 f., Guiraud, *La propriété foncière en Grèce*, pp. 407 ff.

[7] Busolt, pp. 283 f.; Ehrenberg, "Spartiaten und Lazedämonier," in *Hermes*, LIX (1924), 40 ff. The Helots were *δοῦλοι τοῦ κοινοῦ* (Paus. III, 20, 6), *δημόσιοι δοῦλοι* (Ephorus *apud* Strabo VIII, 365); they were assigned to citizens (Herod. IX, 28; Thuc. III, 8) but were not regarded as their property (Arist. *Pol.* 1263a 35) and could neither be sold nor emancipated by the master (Strabo, *loc. cit.*) but only by the state (Thuc. IV, 26, 80; Xen. *Hell.* VI, 5, 28). They were never obligated to deliver more than a fixed amount to their masters (Plut. *Inst. Laced.* 41). Kahrstedt's contention (*Griechisches Staatsrecht*, I, 59, 61 ff.) that the Helots were not bound to the soil and were regarded as private property is answered by Ehrenberg (*loc. cit.*).

[8] Büchsenschütz, *Besitz und Erwerb im Griechischen Altertume*, p. 195; Lauffer, in *Vierteljahrschrift für Sozial- und Wirtschaftsgeschichte*, XXIX (1936), 247 ff. Cf. also Barker, *Greek Political Theory*, p. 323n.

[9] VII, 806de: *γεωργίαι δὲ ἐκδεδομέναι δούλοις ἀπαρχὴν τῶν ἐκ τῆς γῆς ἀποτελοῦσιν ἱκανὴν ἀνθρώποις ζῶσι κοσμίως.*

one part for their slaves, and a third part for the craftsmen, or *metics*, living in the city. The master is to keep only a due proportion for himself and the free members of his family, but the disposal of the whole is in his hands. This regulation obviously puts the agricultural slave in an entirely different position from that which he had in Lacedaemonia, where the amount of his annual payment was fixed, apparently beyond the master's power to alter it, and without regard to the yield in any given year. Under favorable circumstances and with appropriate diligence it was possible for the Helot to acquire considerable property, since he was entitled to all the surplus above the fixed annual rental;[10] whereas the agricultural slave in Plato's state must be content with the amount returned to him by his master. When we recall that Plato rigidly limits the amount of wealth that a *metic* artisan can acquire, and explicitly provides that a freedman shall not be allowed to own more property than his former master, we can readily understand that the relatively independent status of the Lacedaemonian Helot would not accord with his principles.

Again, it is clear that Plato did not intend his agricultural workers to be bound to the soil. The ancestral lot is inalienable; but there is no prohibition on the sale of agricultural slaves in Platonic law, though the law takes notice of traffic in slaves and attempts to provide remedies against fraud (XI, 916a–c). This argument *ex silentio* is supported by the fact that Plato would have his slaves of different nationalities and speaking different languages (VI, 777c). He was opposed, in other words, to any form of slavery which would involve the presence within the city's boundaries of a large homogeneous subject population.[11] The Athenian Stranger specifically mentions the Helots in Lacedaemonia, the Mariandyni in Heraclea, and the Penestae in Thessaly as types of slavery subject to bitter criticism (VI, 776cd), and it is significant that these are all instances of a homogeneous people, once free, who had been reduced to servitude by a conquering race. We can only conclude that Plato did not intend his agricultural slaves to be bound to the soil. For even though originally they were of various alien stocks, yet if attached to the soil

[10] Busolt, p. 669; Plut. *Cleom.* 23. Cf. Glotz, *Le travail dans la Grèce ancienne*, p. 113.

[11] In this judgment he was followed by Aristotle (*Pol.* 1330a 25: τοὺς δὲ γεωργήσοντας μάλιστα μέν, εἰ δεῖ κατ' εὐχήν, δούλους εἶναι, μήτε ὁμοφύλων κτλ. Serfs would necessarily be ὁμόφυλοι. The next best arrangement, according to Aristotle, is to have βάρβαροι περίοικοι to do the work in the fields (1330a 29). Cf. *Econ.* 1344b 18 ff.

from generation to generation they would inevitably become assimilated to one another and possibly also to their masters.[12]

Lastly, the distinction between the agricultural slave and the personal or domestic slave does not appear in Platonic law. There is no distinctive terminology for the agricultural slave, as there was in Crete, Sparta, Thessaly, and everywhere that serfdom existed.[13] Wherever Plato's legislation touches upon the treatment of slaves it ignores any such distinction between the field and the house slave; yet such a distinction must have received legal recognition if it had existed in Plato's state.

If we are to seek historical parallels to Plato's agricultural economy, we should look rather to Attica than to Lacedaemonia. Nothing like the institution of serfdom existed in Attica after the time of Solon. Attic law did not recognize the distinction between agricultural slaves and others. The small proprietor in Attica could not afford to maintain a body of slaves for the exclusive cultivation of his small holdings. The poorest owned no slaves at all. The average proprietor had only one or two slaves, whom he employed in the household or in personal service when there was no work in the fields.[14] A few wealthy country gentlemen maintained elaborate estates, on which large numbers of slaves were employed, and sometimes their management was entrusted to slave overseers. Residing in the city and living from the revenues of their lands, these wealthy owners occupied a position analogous to that of the Spartan citizen.[15] But absentee landlords were the exception at Athens in the fifth century, though such a life did become more common in the fourth century, and was even looked upon in some quarters as the ideal life for the freeman.[16] Did Plato intend that his citizens should live in this fashion, giving all their time to the service of the city, and entrusting the cultivation of their estates to a class of serfs whom they seldom saw? Though some passages in the *Laws* undoubtedly assert that the work of a citizen is enough to absorb all a man's time

---

[12] In the same spirit is Plato's provision limiting the *metic's* period of residence in the state (VIII, 850ab). The result would be to prevent the rise of a large body of native-born but under-privileged persons in the population.

[13] For the equivalence of οἰκέτης and δοῦλος in Plato's law, and the absence of all terms suggestive of serfdom, see note 1 above and Appendix A.

[14] Busolt, pp. 178–179, 762; Glotz, *Le travail dans la Grèce ancienne*, p. 244.

[15] Glotz, *op. cit.*, pp. 302 ff.

[16] Nevertheless Xenophon's praise of the agricultural life in his *Economics* (i–iv) shows that the ideal of the older rural aristocracy was still alive in the fourth century.

(VII, 807a–d; VIII, 835e), yet Plato's legislation is full of indications that he realized the life just described would be impossible for large numbers of his citizens. The poorer classes of citizens are excused from certain public services that may be demanded of the rich, on the ground that they have less leisure to devote to public affairs (VI, 763d; 764a). Again Plato refers to his citizens as tillers of the soil, shepherds, and bee-keepers (VIII, 842d); and gives prescriptions regarding boundaries, pasturage, water supply, and other rural matters on which disputes are likely to arise (VIII, 842e–846d).[17] Thus Plato clearly recognized that his citizens would be compelled, in greater or less degree, to give personal attention to their lots, if not to engage in actual manual labor. It is the Attica, not the Lacedaemonia, of the fifth century that most aptly parallels the life described in the *Laws*.[18]

We can hazard a guess as to the size of the slave population envisaged in the *Laws*. A law we have already cited says that each year the products of the soil are to be divided into three parts—one for citizens, one for their slaves, and one for "all the artisans" (i.e. the foreigners and their slaves). This suggests that the slaves of citizens would be about one-third of the total population and equal in number to the citizen group. To get the total number of slaves, however, we must also add the slaves of the *metics*. It is not likely that the number of slaves owned by metics would be proportionately greater than the number owned by citizens; indeed it is likely to be much less, since the law limits the wealth of the *metic* to an amount considerably below that which a citizen is allowed to acquire. Consequently the number of slaves in the third of the above-mentioned groups would certainly be no more than, and probably much less than, half the total number in the group. Adding these two estimates we get a total slave population of approximately half the total population. This calculation is based on the assumption that the three parts into which the annual produce is divided are approxi-

[17] That these "laws of husbandry" (νόμοι γεωργικοί) are intended to regulate the relations of citizens and not merely the relations of slaves is clear from the fact that the penalties for violating the rules are fines and damages, not stripes. Again in one instance a distinction is drawn between a slave offender and a free offender (845a). Lastly, the institution of the neighborhood courts implies litigation between freemen (XII, 956bc; VI, 762a; XI, 915c).

[18] Bisinger (*Der Agrarstaat in Platons Gesetzen*, p. 84) while asserting that Plato's slave law is devised for "movable slaves," not serfs, looks upon this as an oversight on Plato's part, i.e. Plato failed to realize that the status of slaves in an agrarian economy would be quite different from that of the slaves in an industrial and commercial state like Athens. But it is surely a more plausible explanation to say that Plato was imitating a pre-commercial Attica, where the agricultural population was supposed to be, and for the most part was, a free population.

mately equal, but of course this assumption, though plausible, is not above question. It seems clear on other grounds that Plato was not contemplating a state in which the slave population would be large enough to constitute a standing menace to the supremacy of the free population, as was characteristic of Sparta. In the description of the duties of the ἀγρονόμοι, or rural magistrates (VI, 760–763), no mention is made of the need for watching for sources of disaffection among the slaves and guarding against impending revolts, a duty which we know was an important function of the Spartan κρυπτεία.[19] The general provisions respecting slaves in the *Laws* suggests a situation more comparable to that at Athens, where the slaves were decidedly a minority of the population and consequently not a serious danger in normal times.[20]

From what sources is the slave population to be derived? Piracy and kidnapping were methods much employed in the fifth and fourth centuries for obtaining slaves, but these are strictly forbidden by Plato's law (VII, 823c). Sale into slavery is frequently found in Greek law as a punishment for certain offenses,[21] but this particular penalty does not occur in Platonic law. Nor is there any other way whereby a free man in Plato's state can lose his free status. The children of slave parents were of course slaves according to both Greek and Platonic law;[22] but it is not likely that this method of re-

[19] Though Plato in one passage tentatively gives the name κρυπτεία to these rural police (VI, 763b).

[20] Ridiculously extravagant ideas of the size of the slave population at Athens are still current among the uninformed. Athenaeus' statement (VI, 20) that there were 400,000 slaves in Attica, from which most of the erroneous ideas seem to be derived, was demolished long ago by Hume's criticism ("On the Populousness of Ancient Nations," in *Essays*, I, 418–422). For some recent estimates of the size of the slave population in the late fifth century, see Sargent, R. L., *Size of the Slave Population at Athens*, Urbana, 1925; Tod, M. N., "The Economic Background of the Fifth Century," in *Cambridge Ancient History*, Vol. V; Ehrenberg, V., *Der Griechische und der Hellenistische Staat*, in Gercke and Norden's *Einleitung in die Altertumswissenschaft*, Leipzig, 1932; and Gomme, A. W., *Population of Athens in the Fifth and Fourth Centuries*, Oxford, 1933. These estimates are as follows (in thousands):

	Slaves	*Citizens*	*Metics*
Sargent	67–103	.... 120–208	
Tod	80–120	150–170	35–40
Ehrenberg	80–100	110–125	25–40
Gomme	115	172	28.5

As for Sparta, Ehrenberg estimates the number of citizens (including their families) as between 12,000 and 15,000 for the middle of the fifth century, and the number of Helots somewhere between 140,000 and 200,000.

[21] Chiefly, at Athens, for certain offenses committed by *metics*, such as failure to pay the *metic* tax, or fraudulent enrollment (or attempt at fraudulent enrollment) in the list of citizens. Arist. *Const. of Athens*, XLII, 1; Dem. XXV, 57; Phot. *s.v.* πωληταί; Harpocration, *s.v.* μετοίκιον; Pollux VIII, 99. Elsewhere in Greece it was permitted to sell debtors into slavery, but not in Attica after the time of Solon.

[22] See below, pp. 90 ff.

plenishing the supply of slaves would be much resorted to. It was generally cheaper in the fourth century to buy a grown slave than to breed and rear one in the family; and even if it be assumed that such considerations might not apply to Plato's state, his principle that the slaves in the household should be of diverse nationalities would discourage this method of increase. There remain only capture in war and purchase from slave-traders, and these we may assume to be the means whereby the need for slaves would normally be met in Plato's state.

CHAPTER II

THE RELATION BETWEEN MASTER AND SLAVE

IT IS NATURAL to think of the slave as merely a piece of property and to view his relation to his master as of the same sort as the relation of a cow or a sheep to its owner. This way of thinking was indeed common in fourth-century Greece. Slaves are frequently called ἀνδράποδα, human-footed stock, by analogy with τετράποδα, four-footed stock.[1] Aristotle's characterization of the slave as an "animated tool" is notorious.[2] Plato likewise, in the *Politicus*, defines him as a "species of tame animal," and again as "a servant that is bought and owned."[3] But neither Plato nor Aristotle nor Attic law generally looked upon the slave merely as a piece of property; nor is the relation between master and slave fully described in Greek law by the concept of ownership. This is shown even in terminology, for the slave is more commonly called, not ἀνδράποδον but οἰκέτης (member of the household) or more simply δοῦλος (servant); and likewise the master is not only the owner (ὁ κεκτημένος) but also the lord (ὁ δεσπότης). Looking beyond terminology, we shall find that Attic law treats the slave as owing obligations to persons other than his master, and as a being directly subject to the laws of the city without regard to the will of his master. We shall find that he can be made liable in his own person for offenses, and (more significant still) he is entitled to a certain protection in his own right, both against his master and against other persons. All this shows that the slave in the eyes of the law was in some respects a person (albeit doubtless a very rudimentary one), not merely a kind of livestock. Similarly his relation to his master is held to be, in a real sense, a personal one. The philosophers expressed this aspect of the slave's status in the doctrine that the master's power over his slaves is a species of rule. Thus Aristotle explicitly compares the authority of a master over his household with the rule of a king over his subjects;[4] and Plato refers to the tyrant of a city and the master of slaves as two analogous forms of δυναστεία (VI, 777e). From this point of view the relation between master and slave, though it may result from purchase or bequest or any other process by which ownership is acquired, is

[1] This usage is as old as Homer (*Iliad* VII, 475) and is found in Aristophanes, Thucydides, Plato, Xenophon, Lysias, Demosthenes, and in the inscriptions. Kretschmer in *Glotta*, XVIII (1929), 76. [2] *Pol.* 1253b 32. [3] *Polit.* 289b,d. [4] *Pol.* 1255b 16 ff.; cf. 1252a 7 ff.

distinct from mere ownership in that the personal relation of ruler to subject is involved.

If then we wish to understand Platonic law and Greek law generally on the subject of slavery, we must be careful to keep in mind the dual status of the slave as both a possession and a rudimentary legal person, and the consequent two-fold relation of the master to his slave. The presence of these two aspects of the slave's status introduces a certain complexity and apparent confusion in the law, a confusion that is due to a conflict of principles in the law itself. This being the case, an expositor has no choice but to recognize openly the presence of the two principles, rather than add to the confusion by denying, ignoring, or explaining away attested facts in the interests of a fancied system.[5]

The Slave as Property

> Let all persons abstain, as far as is in their power, from touching anything that is mine, or disturbing the least of my possessions without my consent. And may I likewise, with sound mind, abstain from touching the goods of others (XI, 913a).

This solemn statement of principle shows clearly the intention of Platonic law to give full protection to property rights. It would not be relevant here to go into the details of Plato's law of property. The important parts of this legislation for our purpose are (a) the provision of courts for the settlement of disputes over property (XI, 915c ff.); (b) a system of registration of property, so that disputes as to ownership may in most cases be settled by reference to the register (XI, 914c); and (c) strict regulations regarding buying and selling to prevent fraud and profiteering (XI, 915e–918a). It is

[5] Expositors of Athenian law have been curiously reluctant to admit this duality of principle. The extreme case is Kahrstedt, who insists that Attic law regarded the slave merely as property, and that the power of a master over his slave was absolute (*Staatsgebiet und Staatsangehörige in Athen*, pp. 133 ff., 139 ff., 321–327); but this is to ignore many attested facts and to distort much else. The more usual course is to start, as do Lipsius, Busolt, and Beauchet, from the assumption that Attic law took the slave to be simply property and to regard everything we find that does not fit this assumption as a departure from principle. Thus Lipisus calls the application of the γραφὴ ὕβρεως to attacks upon slaves an *Abfall vom Prinzip* (pp. 793–794). It would be truer to say that there is in this case a conflict of principles, both recognized by the law. The difficulty comes out most clearly and frankly in Beauchet, whose monumental work contains by far the fullest account we have of the Attic law of slavery. Though he lays down the principle that for Attic law the slave was merely a thing susceptible of ownership and therefore without juristic personality, yet he points out that Attic law protects the slave against assaults on his "person" (*Histoire du droit privé de la république athénienne*, II, 423, 426, 428; cf. also p. 401). What is more significant, he treats the law of slavery as a part of the law of the family, which is where it well belongs, though to put it there is hardly consistent with the fundamental principle he has adopted.

made clear in these pages that the slave is considered as property, for there is explicit mention of the procedure for regaining possession of a runaway slave (XI, 914e) and of rules protecting the buyer against deception in the purchase of slaves (XI, 916a ff.). And it is significant that in the latter passage the term ἀνδράποδον is used, which emphasizes of course the property aspect of the slave.

Since then the slave is property, the master as his owner has a legally recognized and protected interest in the slave and in the integrity of his person and powers. It follows that he is entitled to compensation for injury done his slave, just as he is entitled to compensation for damages to any other kind of property. This principle is so familiar and so obvious that we should infer its recognition in Platonic law, even if it did not plainly appear in certain provisions:

> If a man [accidentally] kills a slave [i.e. a slave belonging to another], let him look upon it as if he had destroyed his own. He shall compensate the master of the dead man in full or be subject to a judgment of double the value of the slave (IX, 865c).
>
> If a man kills another's slave in a fit of anger he shall pay the owner double damages (IX, 868a).[6]

These two laws cover two of the forms of homicide recognized in Plato's law.[7] If damages are due in these two cases, *a fortiori* they would be due for deliberate murder. Cases of justifiable homicide are much more complicated, for here the slave has committed an offense, and a new principle comes into operation, viz. the responsibility of the owner for damages done by his property. In such cases, as we shall see later, the master is not entitled to compensation; but the fuller discussion of the master's liability for the unlawful acts of his slaves can be more conveniently taken up later.[8]

The master is also entitled to compensation when his slave is emancipated for services to the state. Platonic law offers freedom to the slave who gives public information of certain offenses, such as appropriating buried treasure (XI, 914a) or mistreating parents (XI, 932d). The law prescribes that in such cases the state shall compensate the owner, unless he happens to be the offender whom

---

[6] The penalty here prescribed is obviously the judgment assessed by the court. If the offender settles out of court he would presumably be expected to pay only the value of the slave, as in the preceding law. On this penalty for litigation, see below, p. 52.

[7] Four forms of homicide were recognized in Platonic law: deliberate or premeditated homicide (φόνος ἑκούσιος, IX, 870 ff.), homicide committed in anger (φόνος θυμῷ πεπραγμένος, IX, 866 ff.), accidental homicide (φόνος ἀκούσιος, IX, 865 ff.) and justifiable homicide (φόνος δίκαιος). Of justifiable homicide there are three sorts mentioned: killing in self-defense or in defense of a near relative (IX, 869cd, 874cd); killing a thief at night (IX, 874bc); and killing for rape or paederasty (IX, 874c).

[8] See below, pp. 59 ff.

the slave has denounced or the person who especially benefits by the prosecution of the offense (XI, 932d).

As a piece of property the slave can be bought and sold under Platonic law. This we learn from the somewhat meticulous provisions for protecting the buyer against the purchase of diseased or ceremonially unclean slaves (XI, 916a–c). No restriction is placed upon the owner's right to sell, other than that he must not deceive the buyer as to the nature of the goods he offers. He must not sell a consumptive, epileptic or diabetic slave, or a homicide, without giving the facts; and if he unwittingly conveys a defective slave he must make restitution.[9] If Plato had intended to impose any restrictions on the right to sell, there would presumably be some penalty here for the attempt to sell property which could not legally be alienated. Nor again is any restriction placed on the right to emancipate, though manumission is dealt with at some length in Platonic law.

These provisions regarding sale and emancipation make it clear that the slave is regarded as private property, not the property of the state; and they make it clear also that Plato is thinking not of the praedial slavery that prevailed in Sparta and Thessaly, but of the industrial and domestic slaves which made up the slave population of Athens. At Sparta the Helots were regarded, not as the property of particular persons, but as the property of the state, being merely assigned to the citizen for his use.[10] The Spartan citizen had no power to sell his slave or to emancipate him, and no right to compensation when the state saw fit to emancipate slaves on its own account. In these respects Plato's law follows the law of his native Athens, which never regarded the slave as anything but private property,[11] and which in the late fifth and fourth centuries became increasingly zealous in protecting the property interests of masters in their slaves.[12]

The master's rights as owner include the right to use his slaves in any lawful way. We get frequent glimpses in the *Laws* of the use to which slaves may be put. They may be employed as physicians for the treatment of other slaves (IV, 720a ff.; IX, 857cd); they may be employed in agriculture (VII, 806d); in personal and domestic service (VII, 805e); as actors (VII, 816e), pedagogues, and teachers

---

[9] For similar regulations at Athens, see Hypereides V, 15.

[10] Strabo VIII, 365; Paus. III, 21, 6, and Busolt, p. 667. See also above, p. 19, note 7.

[11] With the exception, naturally, of the relatively small group of public slaves.

[12] This point is well brought out by Kahrstedt, pp. 139 ff.

, the household described in the *Laws* includes, in the first the son who is destined to inherit the lot and with it the s citizenship, together with the son's wife and children. In the place it includes all other sons of the lot-holder who have not nt abroad as colonists or adopted by some other citizen, and arried daughters. And lastly, it includes the slaves.[20]

e subjects over whom the householder rules, the slaves are hat especially concern us here. The question of the proper s between master and slave seems to have given Plato no ncern, as is evident from the extended passage in Book VI 778a) dealing with the nature and management of slaves. scussion of slavery occurs as part of the regulations regarding e and the establishing of the household, so it is clear that s thinking of the slave primarily in relation to his master t as a person subject to the law of the state.[21] This passage, re, is particularly instructive as to Plato's views of the scope ture of the master's authority. We shall first summarize the ctory parts of this passage, then translate that portion which s Plato's specific recommendations regarding the manage- slaves.

s are a very difficult kind of property, says the Athenian r; they are hard to understand and hard to keep in hand. The opinions are a mixture of truth and falsehood, and the cur- actices in the management of slaves show a mixture of the nt and the inexpedient. Pressed for an explanation of this statement, the Athenian Stranger remarks that the institu- Helotage in Lacedaemonia has caused the most controversy, serting and some denying that it is a happy arrangement ὡς εὖ, τοῖς δ' ὡς οὐκ εὖ γεγονυῖά ἐστιν). The servitude of the

nd insists that there are important differences between the rule of the household e of the state, yet like Plato he looks upon them as two species of the same genus s the authority of the master as a kind of rule (*Pol.* 1252a 7 ff., 1255b 16 ff.). The ption of the household and the position of the master is found in Xenophon (*Cyr.* XXI, especially §§ 10–12).

characteristic of Greek law generally from the earliest period to look upon the istinct from the serf) as a member of the family (Beauchet, II, 394–395; Glotz, 76). An attack upon him was an attack upon his master. His murder was avenged, natural relatives, but by his legal relatives, the family of his master. In the older mission of a newly purchased slave into the family was accompanied by a pleasing The slave was seated at the hearth, where his mistress poured fruits and dried figs ead, a ceremony comparable to that with which a wife or an adopted son was wel- the family.

an *οἰκέτης*, not a δοῦλος, according to the theory of the distinction between these nced by Klaar (*Philol. Wochenschrift*, 1925, pp. 525–528). See Appendix A.

(VII, 808e); and presumably in a great many other occupations and crafts. The law places no limitation upon the right of a *metic* slave-owner to use his slaves in any sort of gainful occupation; but a citizen may not put his slave to work at any handicraft or at retail buying and selling (VIII, 846d, 849c; cf. XI, 920a). This is a striking prohibition which, to my knowledge, has no parallel anywhere else in Greek legislation.[13] It is a forcible expression of Plato's view that industrial and commercial occupations are incompatible with the kind of virtue a citizen should possess, so incompatible that a citizen must not be allowed to engage in them even vicariously through his slaves.

There is a further limitation on the master's use of his slaves in that the state has a right to make use of privately owned slaves in the construction of fortifications, highways, canals, dams, and aqueducts. These constructions are to be carried out under the supervision of the rural magistrates and by the labor of the slaves and domestic animals in the locality affected; but the text adds that they are to be used as much as possible when they are free from "their own work," i.e. from the cultivation of their masters' lots (VI, 760e ff.). Presumably also private slaves would be employed on the public works superintended by the magistrates of the city, such as repairing streets and water supplies (VI, 763cd). It is implied that the owner is not entitled to compensation for the use of his slaves by the state, this being a kind of tax which he can be called upon to pay for public purposes.

In maintaining his rights of ownership, a man may arrest (ἄγειν) any person whom he asserts to be his fugitive slave without court authorization; or anyone else in his family or circle of friends may make this arrest for him (XI, 914e). This is a summary act of self-help, analogous to taking possession of a cow or a sheep over which ownership is claimed (XI, 914cd). This action may be met on behalf of the person arrested by a peculiar procedure, the ἀφαίρεσις εἰς ἐλευθερίαν, which we know of also from Attic law, and which will be studied more fully later.[14] When the status of the arrested person is not in dispute and the question at issue is merely which of two claimants is the owner of the slave, the issue is doubtless to be settled by the same procedure as that prescribed for analogous disputes respecting livestock. First an appeal is made to the public

[13] Certainly not in Attic law. For the use of slaves in industry and trade at Athens, see Westermann, in Pauly-Wissowa, Suppl. VI, 913.

[14] For a fuller discussion of this right of ἄγειν and of the ἀφαίρεσις see below, pp. 111ff.

register of property, and this, in the case of slaves, would doubtless be sufficient, the slave being such a considerable kind of property. But if the matter cannot be thus settled, the property in dispute remains in the possession of the magistrates until ownership has been determined by the courts (XI, 914d).

Lastly, the child of a female slave belongs to her master (XI, 930d). This again is a principle which we meet so often in slave legislation, ancient and modern, that we should infer its recognition in Platonic law even if it were not expressly affirmed. Plato, however, provides that if the slave's master is the father of the child, both child and mother shall be sent out of the land. This is another Platonic innovation whose parallel it would be hard to find. The reasons for it will be discussed later.[15]

The Slave as Subject

In the Platonic writings the household is commonly spoken of as a kind of political community and the master of the household as a species of ruler. These phrases are more than suggestive figures of speech. In the description in Book III of the origin and development of government, the family or household appears as the first political community, with a constitution peculiar to itself which Plato (professing to follow general use) calls a δυναστεία, and which he says is still often found among Greeks and barbarians (III, 680b). The characteristic of this political group is that the head of the household is sovereign: "each man gives laws to his wives and children," as Homer says of the Cyclops. The higher forms of political organization, according to this account, arise from the grouping of families into larger communities, in which, however, the original units persist, with a character and authority of their own. This persistence of the family δυναστεία within the political state is well exemplified in the political structure of the *Laws*. For the state there set up can most aptly be described as a union of households.[16] Its units are not private persons, but lot-holders, each of whom, in relation to his fellow-citizens and the state, stands as the head and representative of a continuing group, while as regards the living members of that group he is, within the limits imposed by the law of the πόλις,

[15] Below, p. 94.

[16] As is shown by the reference in the *Laws* to the "five thousand and forty households" (IX, 877d, XI, 929a). Cf. Aristotle *Pol.* 1253b 2: πᾶσα γάρ σύγκειται πόλις ἐξ οἰκιῶν. Aristotle's account of the origin and composition of the state in the opening chapters of the *Politics* parallels Plato's account in the third book of the *Laws*.

vested with the authority to command a
the point to inquire here into the precise
the family under Platonic law. The vit
relatively independent source of authori
special provisions, for example in the se
try cases of fratricidal strife (IX, 878c
cases of disinheritance (XI, 928e ff.).[17] C
hold is not genuinely sovereign, for the
in its internal affairs. It protects the
parents (IX, 878e) and the parent ag
(XI, 923ab). It settles disputes which
judicate (IX, 878de). It endeavors to
punishment of kin-slayers (a function
prosecuting a delinquent kinsman (IX
most significant of all, it prohibits pr
910cd). We find here, as in Attic law, b
archal authority and family solidari
Greece. Nevertheless, however reduced
mains as a relatively autonomous bod
structure, and the maintenance of its
part of the foundations of social order.

Thus the head of the household is
ruler, and his little domain is a kind c
within the political state. The *Politicu*
ruling a household and the art of ruli
same, the rulers in the two cases bei
number of their subjects (259ab).[19]

[17] Cf. also XII, 954ab (see below, p. 112), where I
ously due to a strong feeling for the position of the h
the citizen's relation to the state and his relation to h
808ab: ἐγειρομένους δὲ νύκτωρ δεῖ πάντας πράττειν τῶ
μικῶν, ἄρχοντας μὲν κατὰ πόλιν, δεσποίνας δὲ καὶ δεσπ
the family bond in early Greece and the nature of
solidarité de la famille dans le droit criminel en Grèce.

[18] This fact is strikingly shown in III, 690a ff.,
seven principles (ἀξιώματα) according to which ru
states and in households" (ἔν τε πόλεσιν μεγάλαις
These principles are: (1) that parents should rule o
birth should rule over commoners; (3) that the eld
masters should rule over slaves; (5) that the strong
wise should rule over the ignorant; (7) that those
those not thus selected. Of this miscellaneous asso
principles of political rule, while others apply only
kinds are necessary for social order.

[19] Though Aristotle protests against Plato's vie

mothe
place,
father
secon
been s
all un
Of
those
relatic
little c
(776b-
This d
marria
Plato
and n
theref
and na
introd
contai
ment c
Slav
Strang
curren
rent p
expedi
cryptic
tion of
some a
(τοῖς μ

two cases
and the r
and rega
same con
I, i; *Econ*
[20] It w
slave (as
pp. 163n,
not by hi
days the
ceremony
upon his
comed in
[21] I.e. a
terms adv

Mariandyni in Heraclea and of the Penestae in Thessaly is mentioned as also subject to criticism.[22] Furthermore, he says, men differ violently in their views as to the nature of slaves. Many praise them as the best and most loyal members of the household—more loyal even than brothers or sons—and point to many instances of slaves saving the lives and property of their masters. Others, following Homer, look upon the slave as only half a man and his soul as utterly unreliable; they use the goad and the whip upon him, as if he were a species of wild beast, and in so doing they make him many times more slave-like than he was before. Man is indeed an intractable creature, and especially so when it comes to maintaining this "necessary distinction" between the slave and the freeman and master. The difficulty of the problem is shown by the frequent revolts among the Messenians and in other places where there are large numbers of slaves speaking the same language; and by the depredations of the so-called "rovers" along the Italian coast.[23]

Anyone who sees all these difficulties will be hard pressed to say what should be done about them. Only two remedies are left us. The first is that those who are to be our slaves shall not come from the same land (μήτε πατριώτας ἀλλήλων εἶναι), but so far as possible shall speak different languages. Thus they will be easier to keep in subjection. The other is to nurture them properly (τρέφειν δ' αὐτοὺς ὀρθῶς), not only for their sakes, but even more for the sake of ourselves. By proper nurture I mean to refrain from all acts of *hybris* (μήτε τινὰ ὕβριν ὑβρίζειν) toward slaves, and if possible, to be more reluctant to wrong them than one's equals. For a genuine and unfeigned love of justice and hatred of injustice is most clearly shown in our relations to those to whom it is easy to be unjust. Whoever in his dealings with his slaves and their acts and dispositions keeps himself 'undefiled' (ἀμίαντος) by violence or injustice (τοῦ τε ἀνοσίου πέρι καὶ ἀδίκου) is best fitted to "sow the seeds of virtue" in them; and this may be said not only of the master but of the tyrant and every other person exercising authority (δυναστείαν δυναστεύοντι) over persons weaker than himself. Slaves must be punished, but justly; and not spoiled by admonition as if they

[22] The Penestae were, in part at least, of Greek stock, earlier inhabitants who had been conquered and reduced to serfdom by the Thessalians, according to Theopompus Fr. 122 (Jacoby). Their condition in some ways was better than that of the Helots, for they could not be put to death without judicial sentence (Athenaeus VI, 264a). They seem also to have been regarded as the property of their masters, not of the state (Dem. XXIII, 199, Xen. *Hell.* II, 3, 36). Like the Helots they could not be sold outside the land. Busolt, p. 1478. The Mariandyni were a barbarian people of northwestern Asia Minor, reduced to serfdom by the Megarian colonists of Heraclea Pontica about the middle of the sixth century. See Ruge, in Pauly-Wissowa, XIV, 1747–1749; Athenaeus VI, 263d; Strabo XII, 542; Pausanias V, 26, 7; Hesychius, *s.v.* δωροφόροι.

[23] "Probably this may be connected with that revolt whereby the Bruttians became enfranchised; but we can make out nothing definite from Plato's language" (Grote, *Plato*, IV 343n).

were free men. One should always address a slave in the language of command. One should not sport or jest with slaves, whether male or female; for though this is often done, it is a senseless practice and its result is to spoil the slave, making his life of servitude more difficult to bear, and the authority of the master harder to maintain (VI, 777c–778a).

Before commenting on Plato's specific proposals, let us direct our attention to certain points in the introductory passage. What is meant by calling the distinction between slave and master a necessary one (VI, 777b)? Some commentators have found in this expression a reluctant concession by Plato to prevailing customs which he would willingly abolish, and even a guarded and cautious assertion of the equality of all men.[24] But the clue to the proper understanding of Plato's thought here is to be found in a passage in Book III affirming the necessity of the distinction between rulers and subjects.[25] The relation between master and slave is one form of the relation between ruler and subject, as this passage asserts. The "necessity" therefore is that masters should rule and slaves obey. When we recall the picture of the ideal ruler drawn in the *Politicus* we can easily understand why Plato should feel that this distinction, though a necessary one, is difficult to maintain, human nature being what it is. The function of the ruler, the *Politicus* tells us, is like that of a shepherd or herdsman. He is the source of commands which his flock must obey, but his end, *qua* ruler, is the good of the flock, not his own private gain. So that in order to fulfill his function a ruler must have knowledge, particularly a knowledge of how to produce virtue in his subjects, for that is their real good. And finally, since his end is the good of his subjects, and since he has knowledge of the proper way to achieve this end, the real ruler (as distinguished from the tyrant or demagogue) is able to enlist the willing obedience of his subjects. Plato could hardly expect his masters to exemplify nothing but disinterested wisdom in the management of their slaves; but some reflection of the ideal must be present if the master's authority is to be maintained. When therefore, Plato says that man is an intractable creature with regard to

[24] Apelt, I, 259, finds here "*eine versteckte Anerkennung der gleichen Menschenwürde*;" and Zimmern, *Greek Commonwealth*, p. 385n, a recognition of "the unity of human nature and the absurdity of dividing off mankind into two separate classes." According to England, Plato is suggesting "that the difficulty has its source in the diversities of a nature which refuses to be forced into our artificial categories" (I, 619).

[25] III, 689e: *ἄρχοντας δὲ δὴ καὶ ἀρχομένους ἀναγκαῖον ἐν ταῖς πόλεσιν εἶναί που.* This statement immediately precedes the enumeration of the seven "axioms" of authority "in cities and in households" referred to above (note 18).

this distinction between slave and master, he is thinking, as England well says, not merely of unwillingness to obey but also of failure of the capacity to rule.[26]

Plato could not fail to be aware, as was Aristotle after him, that some *de facto* slaves are fitted for a better station, and that some actual rulers have the capacity and disposition of slaves.[27] But in principle the authority of the master is regarded by Plato as in accordance with nature and justice. Just as sheep need a shepherd and children need a pedagogue, so slaves need a master (VII, 808d). The nature of the slave is to follow instructions, but not to reason nor to expound (XII, 966b; IV, 720a–c), for he is incapable of apprehending a rational principle (IV, 720a–c). These are passages from the *Laws*, but the same sentiments are found in the other dialogues. The *Republic* asserts that those in whom the "best principle" is lacking or is naturally weak by nature ought to be slaves of those who possess it (IX, 590cd). And in the *Politicus* we are told that the ruling art will put under the yoke of slavery those who are wallowing in ignorance and baseness (309a). There are many references in the dialogues to the slave nature and its intrinsic inferiority to the nature of the free man.[28] In many of these cases the traits referred to as δουλεία are ascribed to men who are free before the law, yet it is obvious that they are regarded as particularly characteristic of slaves in the legal sense of the word. There can therefore be little doubt that Plato was as convinced as Aristotle that the superiority of the freeman to the slave was something more than a legal convention. Since this is so, the subjection of the slave to his master is legitimate. We even find Plato often using the word δουλεία more generally to denote any sort of subjection to legitimate authority, a use which is peculiarly frequent in the *Laws*.[29]

The mention of certain instances of slavery as especially subject to criticism needs comment. Why does the Athenian Stranger select the cases of the Helots, the Mariandyni, and the Penestae for special mention? All of them are examples of serfdom, and in two of them at least the subject population was of Greek stock. Is it the institution of serfdom in general that Plato criticizes, or the enslaving of

---

[26] England, I, 619. For a discussion of this same problem by Xenophon, see *Econ.* XXI. Xenophon concludes that to rule over willing subjects (he is thinking principally of slaves here) requires something like a divine nature.

[27] Like Aristotle (*Pol.* 1255a 25ff.) Plato thinks it wrong to enslave Hellenes (*Rep.* V, 469bc).

[28] *Symp.* 210d; [*Erast.*] 136a; *Theaet.* 173a; *Crito* 52c. See also Xen. *Mem.* IV, ii, 22–23.

[29] See Appendix B.

Greeks? The principle that Greeks should not enslave Greeks is stated in the *Republic* (V, 469bc) and is implied in Aristotle's discussion of slavery (*Politics* 1255a, 25 ff.). No doubt some of the criticism directed at the "peculiar institution" of the Spartans was inspired by this principle. But Plato's opposition seems to be based upon more general grounds. The prime defect in the institution of Helotage was that it involved the attempt to hold in subjection a homogeneous and native population, bound together by the feeling of a common interest and common traditions and a common enmity against their oppressors. To keep such a slave class in subjection required a vast expenditure of time and effort, and an undue development of the military virtues at the expense of the other parts of human excellence.[30] The consequence was that the city was converted into an armed camp, even in times of peace, and the citizen became addicted to violence and brutality.[31] When the Athenian Stranger speaks in a later passage of those masters who use the goad and the whip and thus make their slaves more slave-like than they were before, the reference to the Spartans is unmistakable. As Plutarch says, the slave was more of a slave at Sparta than anywhere else.[32]

The first of Plato's specific proposals is directed against this danger and is equivalent, as we have previously noted, to a rejection of the institution of serfdom, as found in Lacedaemonia and elsewhere. For the requirement that the slaves are to be of different stock and speak different languages would mean a fairly transient slave population, of non-Greek stock. How the requisite turnover in the slave population is to be effected Plato does not say. Perhaps he thought the relative cheapness of bought slaves in comparison with those bred in the household would prevent the multiplication of native-born slaves. In all likelihood this factor produced results at Athens something like those desired by Plato. The use of emancipation, coupled with the peculiar requirement of Plato's law that the freedman must ordinarily leave the country after twenty years, would work toward the same end. One consequence of the rejection of serfdom needs to be noted. However unpleasant the condition of

---

[30] Cf. the criticism of the Spartan training in *Laws* I, 625e ff., 628e, 630d, 634ab.

[31] Thuc. IV, 80, 3, remarks that most Spartan institutions were devised with respect to keeping the Helots in subjection.

[32] *Lycurgus* 28. The overbearing *hybris* of the Spartans and their constant use of the whip on their slaves is recorded by Athenaeus (XIV, 657d). Cf. also Xen. *Hell.* III, 3, 6; *Const. of Lacedaemon* XII, 4; Thuc. IV, 80, 3.

the serf might be, he was, at least at Sparta, in certain respects beyond the control of any private person. He belonged to the community, not merely to a master, and his bondage to the soil meant that he could not be sold away from his native land. Plato's law brings the slaves more completely under the power of their masters, and therefore it is important to see what restrictions in law or morals Plato would place upon this power.

The second of Plato's "remedies" deals with this point. We should note that the proper treatment of his slave by the master is explicitly said to be analogous to the conduct a tyrant should show toward his subjects, or more generally the attitude of any person exercising authority over some one weaker than himself. What this proper treatment is we are told more specifically.[33] The master may and should punish his slave, but he is to punish justly; he is to avoid all *hybris*, and he is to remain undefiled with unholy acts.[34] These statements imply that there are rules of action binding (morally at least) upon the master in his relation to his slaves. It is clear therefore that Plato did not intend the power of a master to take the form of an uncontrolled despotism, but to be a rule over subjects possessing claims which he cannot as a proper ruler ignore. Of these rules binding upon the master Plato says very little, but we may learn something of their content and spirit by inquiring into the meaning of the *hybris* and the "defilement" which Plato solemnly enjoins his masters to avoid.

Hybris was one of the oldest of the Greek moral concepts and was deeply charged with peculiar and powerful associations. It had a place in Attic law,[35] where it was regarded as one of the graver offenses, actionable by a γραφή. A special interest attaches to this prescription in Plato's text because we know that Attic law even permitted the γραφὴ ὕβρεως for attacks upon slaves. But what was the precise nature of the offense? The recorded cases of prosecution for *hybris* under Attic law show the utmost variety.[36] Any sort of bodily injury could apparently furnish the basis for this charge,

[33] The proper τροφή of the slaves implies of course that they should be properly fed. In the division of the annual produce one third is to be set apart for the slaves (VIII, 848a). Cf. the Aristotelian *Economics* 1344a 35 ff. on the importance of food in the management of slaves.

[34] Cf. the law of XI, 914e, which permits a master to punish a runaway slave as he will, but not in anger and not so as to commit "unholiness."

[35] Ὕβρις also figures prominently in Hellenistic law. Cf. the law of Alexandria as given in the *Papyrus Halensis*, lines 210–213 (*Dikaiomata*, p. 107; Meyer, pp. 238 ff.).

[36] On ὕβρις in Attic law see Lipsius, pp. 421–428; Gernet, Louis, *Recherches sur le développement de la pensée juridique et morale en Grèce*, pp. 183–197.

so that it is hard to find any material distinction between ὕβρις and other attacks upon the person, such as αἰκία and φόνος. But *hybris* also included attacks upon the liberty of the person, such as illegal arrest and imprisonment. And there is the famous case of the freedman Phormio being charged with *hybris* for presuming to marry the widow of his former master. The law of *hybris* as given by Demosthenes seems bent on giving the term the widest possible denotation; the offense it denotes seems to be the equivalent of doing any unlawful act.[37] The dramatists likewise use the term to denote a bewildering variety of offenses against religious and moral law, and in the earlier poets βία and ὕβρις seem to be used as simple antitheses of δίκη and εὐνομία. The literary usage thus confirms the conclusion drawn from the evidence of the courts and the lawyers: the concept of *hybris* is broad enough to include all attacks upon the person or the interests of the person.

But it would be a mistake to regard ὕβρις as a simple synonym for injustice; for the term carries a flavor that is absent from ἀδικία. Demosthenes speaks of it as "a kind of action than which there is nothing more to be abhorred or more deserving of anger."[38] When we ask what it is that made *hybris* such a peculiarly abhorrent kind of wrong-doing to the fourth-century Greek, the answer, in part at least, is that it was an affront to the dignity or the honor of the person. Thus Aristotle says that tyrants must be particularly careful to refrain from *hybris* against private persons, for this is a most potent cause of revolutions; and the historical examples that he gives are all cases in which there was an affront to the self-respect or honor of the injured person.[39] Again in the *Rhetoric* he says that *hybris* is not merely striking a man, but striking in order to dishonor him, or to express one's contempt.[40] And Demosthenes asserts that it is not being struck, but being struck ἐφ' ὕβρει, i.e. in such a fashion as to degrade or insult, that is unbearable for a man of honor.[41] Even if the intent to degrade or insult is lacking, an action may be classed as *hybris* if its commission is incompatible with the dignity of the person injured, for instance chastising a free child under the misapprehension that he is a slave.[42]

---

[37] Dem. XXI, 47: ἐάν τις ὑβρίσῃ εἴς τινα, ἢ παῖδα ἢ γυναῖκα ἢ ἄνδρα, τῶν ἐλευθέρων ἢ τῶν δούλων, ἢ παράνομόν τι ποιήσῃ εἰς τούτων τινά, γραφέσθω πρὸς τοὺς θεσμοθέτας ὁ βουλόμενος κτλ. Note the apparent equivalent of the two clauses ἐάν τις ὑβρίσῃ and παράνομόν τι ποιήσῃ. These two clauses are also found in conjunction in Dem. XLIII, 75.

[38] Dem. XXI, 46. [39] *Pol.* 1311a 32 ff.; cf. 1302b 2 ff. [40] *Rhet.* II, 1378b 22 ff.

[41] Dem. XXI, 72. Cf. also the pseudo-Platonic *Definitions*, 415e: ὕβρις ἀδικία πρὸς ἀτιμίαν φέρουσα. [42] Dem. LIII, 16.

It is this meaning of the term that enables us to understand why the orators of the fourth century felt it to be anomalous that the law of *hybris* should apply to attacks upon slaves. For what honor has a slave to lose? Demosthenes argues that one should not consider the person of the injured but the nature of the injury, and remember that nothing is more to be abhorred that *hybris*.[43] Aeschines says that the intention of the law was not so much to protect the slave as to habituate the citizens to the kind of mutual self-respect necessary in a democracy. "For whoever commits *hybris* at all, against any person whatever (εἰς ὀντινοῦν) is not fit to be a fellow-citizen in a democracy."[44] Both these explanations, it will be observed, explain the anomaly only by admitting that it was not an anomaly, that is, by asserting that *hybris* toward slaves was really possible. We should be more inclined to-day to find the key to the dilemma in a change in the nature of the slave class which had occurred between the formulation of this law and the time of Demosthenes.[45] The law expresses the attitude characteristic of the earlier time when most of the slaves were of Greek blood and employed in domestic service or in agricultural tasks on small estates. In the fourth century most of the slaves in Athens were of barbarian origin, and the growth of commerce and industry had brought in large numbers whose relations to their masters were in some respects as impersonal as the relations of employees to their employer in modern industry. Under these circumstances the sense of the "personality" of the slave was less likely to be aroused.

Yet the feeling of the slave's membership in the community of persons was still alive in the fourth century, as the arguments of the orators show. There were certain special occasions when the sense of *hybris* seems to have been peculiarly strong. Many of the cases of *hybris* occurring in Attic literature are outrages committed against weaker persons, such as women, children, foreigners, or slaves.[46] Since these persons were often completely incompetent to bring legal action in their own behalf, and nearly always legally

---

[43] Dem. XXI, 46.

[44] *Timarchus* 17. Compare this reasoning with Plato's assertion that we should treat our slaves rightly, not only for their sakes, but also (and chiefly) for our own.

[45] It seems clear that the law of ὕβρις was old; in all likelihood it was a part of the legislation of Solon. See the author's "Murder of Slaves in Attic Law," *Class. Phil.* XXXII (1937), 226.

[46] For example, the attack upon the child in Dem. LIII, 16; the assault on the Rhodian maiden in Dinarchus *Demosthenes*, 23. The marriage of Phormio, the freedman, with the widow of his former master is probably also a case in point, since he was her κύριος.

inferior, they were especially exposed to insult and injury. It is for this reason that the ancient law made the offense actionable by a γραφή, thus providing a legal way of punishing wrongs committed against persons who could not protect themselves.[47] This law, when we consider its intent, must be regarded as one of the most enlightened parts of Athenian legislation, and it shows how severely an outrage upon a weaker member of the community could be condemned. Furthermore, Gernet has called attention to the fact that the public sense of *hybris* was purest and most intense when an outrage had been committed upon an individual at a religious ceremony.[48] Thus, for example, a certain Themistius of the Attic deme of Aphidna was put to death for assaulting a Rhodian harp-player at an Eleusinian festival.[49] The interpretation to be placed upon this phenomenon seems fairly obvious. The weaker persons in the community, though not counted as citizens nor as sharers in the law, in the strict sense of the word, were still regarded as members of the religious community. And the sense of their right to protection would be peculiarly strong when the religious sentiments were aroused.[50]

In the light of these considerations, Plato's injunction assumes considerable significance. It is not merely an injunction to avoid injustice toward slaves; it is a recognition of something like personal dignity in the slave, and an assertion that the slave's person must be respected, despite (and perhaps also because of) his weaker position. And it implies also that the slave, in spite of his vulnerable legal status, is to be regarded as protected by the sanctions of morality and religion. It is very doubtful whether Plato would follow Attic law in permitting the prosecution of a master guilty of *hybris* toward his slave (we shall inquire into this later), but there can be no doubt that it was his intention to impress upon his

[47] One is almost tempted to say that the term ὕβρις originally meant an offense against a weaker person. Thus in Plato's text the prohibition of ὕβρις is followed at once by what would seem to be regarded as its equivalent, viz. an exhortation to avoid injustice to those "to whom it is easy to be unjust." Cf. also *Laws* III, 691c; IV, 716a. Of course the term was used more broadly than this in the fourth century, at least in the law of Alexandria.

[48] *Op. cit.*, pp. 189 ff. [49] Dinarchus, *Demosthenes* 23.

[50] Many Athenian customs bear witness to the fact that the religious community was broader than the political. Although slaves were excluded from the assembly and from the gymnasia and palaestrae, which were reserved for citizens, yet they were ordinarily admitted to religious ceremonies and public sacrifices. Slaves could be members of the religious brotherhoods, or θίασοι, along with free men, and those of Greek blood could even be initiated into the Eleusinian mysteries. For the sources, see Beauchet II, 424. There is nothing in Plato's regulations pertaining to religious ceremonies upon which we can base a clear inference regarding the slave's place in these ceremonies.

masters in as solemn a manner as possible the obligations of self-restraint. Not that the dignity of the slave's person was the chief object of Plato's solicitude here. On the contrary, he says we must treat our slaves properly, not merely for their sakes but chiefly for the sake of ourselves. The crime of *hybris* in other words, can be looked at from two points of view, as an injury or insult to the person who suffers, or as lack of self-control in the person who does the injury. And it is the latter aspect of the offense which seems to bulk largest in Plato's thought, both here and elsewhere in the *Laws*.[51] His attitude would seem to be identical with that expressed by the orator Aeschines in a passage quoted above, that the disposition to commit *hybris* unfits a man for citizenship in a society of free men.

The master is further enjoined to avoid all "unholiness" in his treatment of his slaves. Is this addition significant? The phrase δίκαιον καὶ ὅσιον is not a redundancy, either in Platonic or in Attic law. It seems to be the precise analogue of the Roman *jus et fas*. "Unholiness" is a violation of certain rules of conduct peculiarly sanctioned by religious sentiments, even though legal sanctions be lacking. Incest and bloodshed, especially fratricidal bloodshed, are the two crimes most often referred to in Plato as unholy.[52] Of the two it is only bloodshed which comes in question when the relation of master and slave is concerned; so that the practical import of Plato's exhortation to his masters to remain "undefiled" is to avoid violence and bloodshed in the handling of slaves. It was a belief, common in Greece from at least the seventh century onward, that the shedding of blood involved pollution, a pollution which could be wiped out only by the performance of certain ceremonial rites. There are frequent references to these ceremonies of purification in Plato's law of homicide, and as we shall see more fully later, these requirements of purification are imposed upon the killer of a slave as upon any other homicide. These rules were essentially of religious origin, as was the conception of the horror of bloodshed in which

---

[51] This is particularly evident when ὕβρις is connected, not with ἀδικία (as in I, 630b; II, 662a; III, 679c, 691c; X, 906a) but with some form of ἀκολασία (I, 649d; VI, 783a; X, 884). For ἀδικία καὶ ὕβρις elsewhere in Plato see *Soph.* 229a, *Polit.* 309a. For ὕβρις καὶ ἀκολασία, *Phaedr.* 253e, *Gorg.* 525a, *Rep.* III, 403a, VIII, 560e, *Phaed.* 81e, *Apol.* 26e.

[52] Incest and licentiousness are called unholy in *Laws* VIII, 838b, 840d; *Rep.* V, 458e. Fratricidal bloodshed in *Laws* IX, 877e, *Rep.* X, 615cd; *Ep.* VII, 334a. Neglect of filial duties in *Rep.* V, 463d. It is significant that these are all offenses within the family and thus peculiarly subject to religious, rather than to political sanction. The phrase δίκαιον καὶ ὅσιον is almost a cliché in Plato. Cf. *Laws* II, 663b, d, VIII, 840d; XII, 959b; *Polit.* 301d; *Gorg.* 507b; *Rep.* I, 331a; X, 615b; *Theaet.* 176b. *Prot.* 325d gives us the trio δίκαιον, καλόν, ὅσιον.

they are rooted; and they were interpreted and administered by the Delphian Apollo, rather than as laws of the city-state. Yet even so, they were a powerful instrument of social control and even affected in important respects the Athenian law of homicide. Plato, then, is using no idle form of words when he enjoins his masters to refrain from unholy acts. They carry the implication that the slave, as well as the free man, is under the protection of the Delphian Apollo, and must be regarded as something more than a beast of burden whose blood can be shed without shame or pollution.

Thus the master in Plato's state is subject to certain restraints in the exercise of authority over his slaves. But we must be on our guard against misunderstanding the nature of these restraints. In the passage under examination, the obligations Plato imposes upon the master are obligations of conscience, not legal obligations which he can be compelled to perform by the city's courts. Whether or not in exceptional cases there are legal obligations laid upon the master with respect to the person of his slave we shall examine in a later chapter. Here we can only call attention to the fact that the "justice" which the slave gets from his master need not by any means be the same as the justice which one citizen can demand of another in the law courts. The situation can be made clear by appealing to a distinction drawn by Aristotle between "household justice" and political justice. Political justice is action in accordance with the laws of a political community of free and equal persons. Household justice is like political justice, though "not the same," says Aristotle.[53] The difference would seem to be, not that household justice lacks principles or rules, but that the persons whose relations are regulated by it do not enjoy that reciprocity of ruling and being ruled which characterizes the free and equal citizens of a state.[54] And a consequence is that the ruler in a household can with more impunity violate the rules of household justice than the ruler in a state can violate the city's laws. It is evident that it is household justice, in Aristotle's sense of the word, that regulates the relation of the master to his slave in Plato's state. The master of the household is explicitly compared to a tyrant and is said to exercise δυναστεία towards persons weaker than himself. This term is used by Plato elsewhere, as we have already observed, to denote the constitution of the family, considered as a primitive political group, in which the word of the head is law (III, 680b); and in all its uses in Greek

[53] *Nic. Eth.* V, 1134b 8 ff. [54] *Ibid.* 1134b 14.

literature the term seems to imply personal and irresponsible power.[55] It is all too evident why Plato should exhort his masters to be especially careful to do justice to their slaves, because they are persons toward whom it is easy to be unjust.

One is tempted to speculate why Plato, who saw that his earlier ideal of a ruler untrammelled by law is too high for human nature and that justice requires the introduction of laws to prevent the misuse of political power, did not also see that law is necessary to prevent the abuse of power by masters. If all ruling is the same in principle, as Plato declared in the *Politicus*, then the necessity of constitutional rule in the political community would imply something analogous in the household; i.e. some legislation protecting the slave against abuse by a master upon whom the obligations of morality and religion might weigh lightly. Such legislation would have been in full accord with tendencies already manifest in Greek law, as shown for example in the law of Athens and the law of Gortyn. But though Plato's law is lofty in its intentions, we cannot say that it makes it any less easy for a master to be unjust to his slaves. It is, of course the purpose of the institutions described in the *Laws* to train the citizens in the virtues that a ruler and householder must possess, and it might be said that if these institutions accomplish their end there will be no need of legislation. But the same observation could be made of any field in which legislation enters to correct the occasional offender upon whom the processes of moral education have not taken effect, and it hardly excuses Plato's failure to do here what he did in so many other cases, viz. add the sanctions of law to the obligations of morality.

Let us turn now to the positive duties which a master owes his slaves. Plato recognizes it as one of the responsibilities of the master to "sow the seeds of virtue" in his slaves, first by his own example of unfailing justice and propriety in his treatment of them, and second by direct instruction. This is an echo of the doctrine of the *Politicus*, where the ideal ruler is said to have the knowledge of how to produce virtue in his subjects. Elsewhere in the *Laws* we read of the moral education of slaves. The slave is to be taught the fundamentals of the moral law, e.g. that incest is unholy and that the

[55] Busolt, p. 358. Cf. Arist. *Pol.* 1272b 1 ff., 1292b 5 ff., and 1293a 30 where the term means arbitrary power not subject to law. In Plato *Theaet.* 176c it is used generally to mean simply "government"; in *Polit.* it denotes oligarchy, as in Thucydides III, 62, 3 (and possibly also IV, 78, 3). In *Rep.* VIII, 544d it denotes a nondescript kind of government; such δυναστεῖαι are coupled with ὠνηταὶ βασιλεῖαι.

just life is the holiest and happiest (VIII, 838d; II, 664b, 665a). Again, slave children are to be educated along with free children, up to the age of six years at least (VII, 794b). And slaves are to take part in the choric festivals, which have a decidedly educational function in Plato's state (II, 665c; VII, 817e). The rules of censorship apply to the making and reading of poetry by slaves as well as by freemen (XI, 936a). (The purpose of these rules, of course, is to safeguard the character of those who are exposed to the influence of the poetic art.) The implication of all these provisions is that the slave has a nature which is capable of understanding and obeying certain parts at least of the moral law, and it is the responsibility of the master to make of it the best that it is capable of becoming. This teaching of Plato should be compared with a similar doctrine in Aristotle, who says that the master should be the "source of excellence" in his slaves, and not merely possess the art of directing them in their labor.[56] Aristotle explicitly distinguishes between the virtue of the slave and the virtue of the freeman, the former consisting in the capacity to acquire courage and temperance, enough at least to prevent him from failing in his duty through cowardice or lack of self-control. The same distinction is implicit in Plato; for it is plain from the above passages that courage and temperance are precisely the virtues that Plato thinks the slave can be taught.[57] The higher virtue of wisdom he would believe, with Aristotle, can be attained only by the freeman.

We come now to the last and most striking of Plato's prescriptions regarding the treatment of slaves, those that require the masters always to address their slaves in the language of command, to punish and not admonish them, and to refrain from all joking or camaraderie with their slaves. Aristotle saw fit to criticize this part of Plato's teaching, because, he said, slaves have more need of admonition than free men.[58] But Aristotle's criticism rests upon a misunderstanding. If these clauses be taken, as Aristotle evidently took them, to forbid all moral instruction of slaves otherwise than through the power of example, then Plato's prescriptions here are inconsistent with the provisions we have cited in the preceding paragraph. But Aristotle's reading of this passage was somewhat hasty. The admonition (μὴ νουθετοῦντας κτλ) that Plato forbids is

[56] *Pol.* 1260a 33 ff.

[57] The slave virtues praised in VI, 776d are evidently courage and loyalty. Of course both Plato and Aristotle would look upon the courage of the slave as inferior to the courage of the freeman. For Plato's view see *Rep.* IV, 430b.

[58] *Pol.* 1260b 5.

not the admonition used for instruction, but the admonition or "warning" that is often given the freeman in the place of punishment when he has violated a law.[59] Plato means to say that the slave is to be punished (i.e. in his body) when he has done wrong; the monitory type of punishment is suited only to freemen. This may seem a harsh measure of discipline, but obviously it does not exclude all admonition and moral instruction; and we have just seen that Plato intends that the slave shall receive moral instruction. It appears that the general purpose of these provisions is to maintain in as sharp a fashion as possible the distinction between master and slave, i.e. between ruler and subject. They reflect, undoubtedly, Plato's view of the vast difference between the slave nature and the free. But they should also be taken, I believe, as a prudent device for maintaining authority in a society where the rulers of the household are not always and obviously superior to those they rule; and this we may believe Plato thought might be true of his own state, despite the best efforts of educators and legislators.[60]

It is not difficult to see in these prescriptions an implied criticism of the policy of most Athenian masters. The condition of the slaves at Athens seems to have been an exceedingly happy one. We know from many sources that the Athenians treated their slaves, whether from humanity or from shrewd considerations of policy, with considerable leniency, or as Plato would doubtless regard it, with extreme laxness. The Old Oligarch tells us, among other things, that at Athens citizens and slaves were indistinguishable in appearance, that slaves lived in luxury and stood in awe of nobody, and that in short the utmost lack of discipline (ἡ πλείστη ἀκολασία) prevailed.[61] Greek comedy gives us many instances of the sort of familiarity between master and slave which Plato must have had in mind.[62] The mingling of ranks in a democracy is the object of his

---

[59] As in VIII, 845b, where the slave is to be punished with stripes (πληγαῖς κολάζειν), the freeman is to be warned (ἀποπέμπειν νουθετήσαντα); cf. *Ep. VII*, 331b.

[60] These provisions may instructively be compared with those contained in the treatise on Economics which comes, if not from Aristotle, at least from an early Peripatetic. The intercourse of a master with his slaves should be such as not either to allow them to be insolent or to irritate them. They should be given wine very rarely, but should receive work, punishment, and food in due measure. As incentives to "virtue" the slave should be offered rewards, such as clothing, leisure, amusement, marriage, and finally freedom at a specified date. *Economics* 1344a 29 ff.

[61] [Xen.] *Const. of Athens* I, 10; cf. also Dem. *Phil.* III, 3; Aeschines *Timarchus*, 54, 79; Aristophanes *Eccles.* 721–722, Plautus *Stichus*, 447–460.

[62] Such as the behavior of Xanthias in the *Frogs*, Cario in the *Plutus*, Sosion and Xanthias in the *Wasps* of Aristophanes.

bitter satire in the *Republic*, and the anomalous position of the slave does not escape his notice. The last extreme of liberty is reached, he says, when the bought slave is as free as his master (*Rep.* VIII, 563b). He even ridicules the freedman who, having just been emancipated, goes to marry his master's daughter (*Rep.* VI, 495e). The really cultured man, he says in another connection, will despise his slaves and not condescend even to speak harshly to them, unlike the timocratic man, who will be "rough with slaves," Plato tells us, though courteous with freemen (*Rep.* VIII, 549a). The authority of a master over his slaves was duly recognized in Athenian law, but Athenian practice seems usually to have been much milder than the law. Plato therefore would improve upon Athenian policy by taking this distinction in earnest and making the manners and customs conform. At the same time he would insist that the slave, however different in nature from the free man, and however subject legally to his master's power, was entitled to a stern sort of justice.

Chapter III

THE PROTECTION OF THE SLAVE'S PERSON

As a piece of property, and sometimes a very valuable one, the slave is naturally protected by the law and by the remedies the law provides whereby an owner can recover for damages done to his property. But is the slave also entitled in his own right to protection from malicious injury to life and limb?

Injuries to the person are divided by Platonic law into three main classes: αἰκία, assault without bodily injury; τραῦμα, wounding; and φόνος, homicide. Plato's law contains no provisions for the protection of slaves against αἰκία and τραῦμα, though the prescriptions governing such offenses against free persons are systematic and detailed (IX, 879b ff.). The silence of Plato's law here has its parallel in the Alexandrian law of the *Papyrus Halensis*, which deals with αἰκία (in Alexandrian law called ὕβρις) on free persons, but makes no mention of αἰκία on slaves. On the other hand, Attic law seems to have given some protection to the slave against assault, and the law of Gortyn likewise.[1] Either then Platonic law is accidentally incomplete (as the *Papyrus Halensis* probably is), or it falls short of the humanity observable in both Attic law and the law of Gortyn. The latter alternative is at least suggested by the fact (which will be commented on in the next chapter) that the summary flogging of offending slaves by free persons is not only permitted but sometimes enjoined by Plato's law, whereas under the law of Alexandria and Athens such punishment is inflicted by and under the direction of the magistrates. To permit any free person to exercise the authority of a magistrate to punish the delicts of slaves is to render the slave's person exceedingly vulnerable in practice, even if in principle it is regarded as entitled to protection.

There is one injunction in Platonic law that would seem to afford protection to the slave's person as such, viz. the prohibition of *hybris* towards slaves (VI, 777d). We have already discussed the

[1] The statement of the Old Oligarch (Xen. *Const. of Athens* I, 10) that at Athens it was not permitted to strike a slave shows that some protection was given the slave's person by law. This must mean at the least that no one could strike another's slave with impunity. Whether in such cases the master could bring a δίκη αἰκίας against the offender, as Lipsius infers (p. 428), or was limited to the γραφὴ ὕβρεως, as Beauchet maintains (II, 431, n. 2), is uncertain. The law of Gortyn prescribes fines for assaults by free persons upon slaves (Col. II, lines 7–16; Bücheler-Zitelmann, pp. 19, 101 ff.).

nature of the offense so called and have found that the concept of *hybris* was broad enough to include any attack upon the individual, and had special reference to the kind of attack that involves humiliation and degradation. Thus we found it to be a recognition of the slave's person as deserving of protection in its own right. We saw also that *hybris* was a wrong in Attic law which could be proceeded against by a γραφή, that is, the offender could be prosecuted by any citizen, not merely by the injured party or his representative. Furthermore, the γραφὴ ὕβρεως would serve to bring the suit before a heliastic court; and since the charge was a very broad one, the γραφὴ ὕβρεως could evidently be used to punish any kind of mistreatment of slaves contrary to the popular sense of what was right and fitting. Thus it would seem that this provision of Attic law was capable of affording considerable protection to the slave.[2] But the γραφὴ ὕβρεως is nowhere mentioned nor even suggested in the *Laws*, though the procedure of the γραφή is recognized. Nor is any other legal procedure provided for prosecuting a person guilty of mistreating a slave, other than the suits for damages which lie within the competence of the master. It would seem that Plato's injunction against *hybris* is moral only, without legal import or sanctions.

By contrast with the silence of Plato's law respecting other offenses against slaves, his law regarding homicide is comparatively full and explicit. The chief provisions are as follows:

(a) Accidental killing:

If any man kills a slave, let him look upon it as if he had destroyed his own, and let him recompense the dead man's master in full, or be subject to a judgment of double the value of the dead slave. The value shall be set by the judges. The purifications shall be greater and more numerous than those required of him who has killed another (i.e. a freeman) in the games (IX, 865a).

If a man kills his own slave, let him purify himself according to the law and be quit of the homicide (IX, 865d).

[2] Whether it actually did so in practice may well be doubted. For it was a rule of Attic law that a person bringing a γραφή must receive one-fifth of the votes of the court or be liable to a fine of a thousand drachmae (Bonner and Smith, II, 56; Dem. XXI, 47; LVIII, 6; Andoc. IV, 18; Plato *Apol.* 36ab). The risk involved in bringing such a suit would therefore be great, unless the facts could be easily established and the offense was a very grave one. Nevertheless Demosthenes tells us that some men had paid the penalty of death for *hybris* against slaves (XXI, 49). See the author's article, "Murder of Slaves in Attic Law," in *Class. Phil.* XXXII (1937), 217 ff. The application of the γραφὴ ὕβρεως to attacks upon slaves is clearly shown in the text of the law given by Demosthenes XXI, 47 (cited above, p. 38n); and this is confirmed by Athenaeus (VI, 666 f.) who cites as his authorities Demosthenes (as above) and also Lycurgus and Hyperides in orations that have been lost. Cf. also Aeschines *Timarchus* 15.

(b) Homicide committed in anger:

> If any man kills a slave, if it be his own, he shall purify himself; if it be another's, he shall pay the owner double damages (IX, 868a).

(c) Deliberate homicide. After prescribing the penalty and procedure for deliberate murder of citizen by citizen (viz. death and non-burial in the land, IX, 871a–872a), the law declares:

> The same shall hold of the murder of a stranger by a citizen, or a citizen by a stranger, or a stranger by a stranger, or a slave by a slave (IX, 872a).

Then follows, after an interval, this ambiguous declaration:

> If any man kills a slave that has done no wrong, but out of fear that he may inform the magistrates of his misdeeds, or for any other reason of this sort, then let him be liable to prosecution for the murder of such a slave in the same way as he would have been prosecuted if he had killed a citizen (IX, 872c).

The first point to note is that in all these cases the homicide is required to undergo "purification." This is explicitly prescribed in the text of the first three laws quoted; in the other cases it is not necessary to prescribe it explicitly, for deliberate murder carries with it greater defilement than any other kind (IX, 871a), and in any case a *δίκη φόνου* in Attic law always began with a public announcement (*πρόρρησις*) implying the pollution of the accused. The details of this purification, Plato elsewhere tells us, are to be prescribed by the *Exegetes* (IX, 865d, XI, 916c), according to "the law brought from Delphi" (IX, 865b). The ceremonial acts required vary with the circumstance of the homicide. Thus "greater and more numerous purifications" are required of the killer of a slave than of the killer of a competitor in the games. The "purifications" required for the accidental killing of a slave are the same as for the accidental killing of a freeman. Purification is required not only of the murderer of a slave, but also of a slave guilty of bloodshed; for we learn from XI 916c, that a slave homicide carries defilement with him and penalties are prescribed for selling a slave thus defiled.

What is the meaning of this purification required in Plato's law? We have already referred to the belief, common in Greece from at least the seventh century, that the shedding of blood involved pollution, a pollution which, if not removed, would bring disaster upon the family of the murderer or upon the community in which he resided.[3] That this doctrine had not always been held by the Greeks

[3] Bonner and Smith, I, 53 ff.; Treston, *Poine: A Study in Ancient Greek Blood-Vengeance.*

is shown by the Homeric poems, which contain no trace of it. The coming of this doctrine into Greece produced a double change in the punishment of homicide: composition was no longer permitted, as in Homeric days, and the removal of the defilment became the concern of the community as well as of the family. This doctrine had the powerful support of the Delphian Apollo, to whose *exegetes* the interpretation of the "law of purification" was entrusted in historical times. Essentially a religious law, and thus not limited to the city-state nor deriving its sanction from the political officials, it nevertheless affected the homicide law of Athens. One effect is shown in the ancient procedure used in trials for homicide, particularly in the requirement that such trials should take place in the open air, so as to diminish the danger of pollution through association with the slayer. Another effect is shown in the legal consequences of the πρόρρησις, or public notice addressed to the slayer at the beginning of legal action against him, warning him to absent himself from the temples, the agora, and other public places. It appears that anyone who violated these prohibitions would be liable to an action for impiety or to summary arrest by any private person.[4] More than this, the πρόρρησις cast a presumption of guilt upon the accused, and doubtless hampered him greatly in the making of his defense. Perhaps this is why we hear of so few trials for homicide at Athens. The accused, finding himself under the handicap of being presumed guilty until he had proved his innocence, would in many cases use his privilege of fleeing the country rather than stay and attempt to prove his innocence.

This is the doctrine of pollution that figures so prominently in the Platonic law of homicide.[5] Its presence in Plato's legislation has a peculiar significance in respect to the status of the slave. No such ceremonial purification was required for the killing of an ox or a sheep. The slave, then, was something more than a piece of property, an "animated tool." He was a member of the community of persons, whose blood, protected by the gods, could not be shed without exposing the family and the community to disaster. Thus before the demands of this religious doctrine the distinction between slave and freeman tends to disappear; and in one case, as we have seen, it is

---

[4] Bonner and Smith, II, 213 f.

[5] Besides the passages already quoted, the doctrine of purgation is referred to in IX, 872e ff.; XI, 916cd; V, 735d ff. Cf. also VI, 759c. The πρόρρησις, specifically mentioning the places the slayer is not to visit, occurs in IX, 868a, 871a, 873b.

explicitly said that the shedding of slave-blood involves as much defilement as the killing of a freeman (IX, 865d).[6]

But this was religious law. Let us turn to the more strictly civil penalties imposed for the murder of a slave. It would seem that the killing of a slave without legal authority (except in cases of justifiable or excusable homicide)[7] is contrary, not only to religious, but also to civil law. This is not explicitly stated, but may be inferred from the incidental reference to the fact that a slave who has murdered his master is entitled to trial (IX, 872b).[8] This would imply that it was unlawful to put such a slave to death without judicial sentence. And if it was illegal to put a slave to death under these circumstances *a fortiori* it would be unlawful to put him to death for lesser offenses.

This principle was certainly valid in Attic law. It is attested by Antiphon that the deliberate killing of a slave without judicial authorization was, and had long been, contrary to the laws of Athens. In the *Murder of Herodes* Euxitheus condemns his accusers for putting to death the slave whom they had questioned. It was not for them, he says, but for the Athenian people to judge whether a man deserved to die, and it was for the magistrates of the Athenians to execute the sentence. They have therefore usurped the function of both judges and executioners, and in so doing have violated their "ancestral laws."[9] Lycurgus remarks that the "ancient lawgivers" (by which Draco is certainly meant) "did not permit even the killer of a slave to escape with a fine."[10] A law of Solon prescribed that there should be judicial procedure for the murder of a slave as for the murder of a freeman.[11] Thus Antiphon would seem to have been justified in saying that this principle belonged to the πάτριοι νόμοι. In the fourth century it seems to have been widely embodied in the codes of other Greek cities, to judge from Isocrates' statement that apart from Sparta, where the ephors had the power of life and death, it was not lawful to put to death even the most worthless slave without a trial.[12]

But we must carefully distinguish between declarations of legal principles and the remedies available for punishing violations. When

---

[6] The same requirement of purification for the killing of a slave occurs in Attic law. Antiphon VI, 4.

[7] For the forms of justifiable homicide recognized in Platonic law, see above, p. 27n.

[8] IX, 872b: ἐὰν δὲ δοῦλος . . . ἀποκτείνῃ καὶ ὄφλῃ τὴν δίκην κτλ.

[9] V, 47, 48. [10] *Leocrates* 65.

[11] *IJG*, II, xxi, 36: κατὰ ταὐτὰ φόνο δίκας εἶναι δõλον κτέναντι ἒ ἐλεύθερον.

[12] *Panath.*, 181: τοῖς ἄλλοις Ἕλλησιν οὐδὲ τοὺς πονηροτάτους τῶν οἰκετῶν ὅσιόν ἐστι μιαιφονεῖν.

we examine Platonic law with this distinction in mind, we find few penalties imposed for the killing of slaves. For accidental killing nothing is required of the killer except to compensate the owner. But killing in anger does involve a certain degree of guilt in Plato's law, though not as much as deliberate murder;[13] and for this we would expect a penalty. Platonic law prescribes that a man who kills a slave in anger is required to pay the owner double the value of the slave. Here indeed we have punitive, as well as compensatory damages. But for what offense are these extra damages imposed? Are they a punishment for the killing of the slave, or a penalty for failing to settle amicably out of court? Against the former alternative is the fact that no penalty (other than purification) is imposed upon the man who kills his own slave in anger. For the latter view we have the analogy of the law of accidental killing, which clearly means that if a man settles for the slave out of court he pays only the value of the slave; but if he waits for a judgment of the court against himself, then he must pay double. This penalty of litigation frequently occurs in Platonic law, and in Greek law generally.[14] We may take it, then, that this law prescribes no penalty, strictly speaking, for the murder of the slave; it prescribes only a penalty for litigation.

The deliberate murder of a slave by a slave is punished by death and non-burial (IX, 872a–b). As to the deliberate murder of a slave by a freeman we have the above-mentioned ambiguous law of 872c. Ritter, in his note on this passage,[15] interprets it as meaning that the punishment for the deliberate killing of a slave shall be the same as for the deliberate killing of a citizen. He argues that Plato has previously (IX, 870a–e) listed three motives for murder, viz. desire for money, ambition or jealousy, and fear of exposure; and that of these three motives the last (the one mentioned in this law) is the only one that could ordinarily lead to the murder of a slave. Therefore he concludes that Plato intends this law to cover all cases of deliberate murder of slaves. But against this view it can be argued that if Plato had intended to assimilate the deliberate murder of a slave to all other kinds of deliberate murder, he could have done this much more simply and naturally, by annexing, to the list of the cases given in 872a, the simple clause "or the murder of a slave by a freeman."

[13] *φόνος θυμῷ πεπραγμένος* was an innovation of Plato's; Attic law distinguished only *φόνος ἑκούσιος* and *φόνος ἀκούσιος*. For Plato's treatment of this form of homicide see IX, 863 ff., especially 866d ff.

[14] XII, 946e, 954b, 956cd. For Greek law generally see Partsch, *Archiv*, VI, 70.

[15] P. 289.

Since the law of 872a precedes the law now under discussion by only a few lines; since it is so meticulous in distinguishing the various cases which the law is to cover; and since, though slaves are mentioned, the law prescribes a penalty only for the murder of slave by slave, the inference is unavoidable that Plato did not intend this law to apply to the murder of a slave by a freeman. If (which is improbable) there was an accidental omission in 872a and the purpose of 872c was to fill in the gap thus left in the previous law, there was little point in mentioning the special case of murder committed from fear of exposure. The fact that this special kind of murder is singled out for mention is most naturally taken to mean that Plato is here only concerned to penalize offenses of this specific sort.

It is not difficult to imagine why Plato should be particularly concerned with this kind of case. As we shall see later, Plato attached great importance to the function of slave informers in the administration of justice.[16] A guilty master, knowing that his slave knew of his misdeeds and possessed the right to lay information before the magistrates, would certainly be inclined to make away with this dangerous individual. There are hints in the literary tradition that this sometimes happened at Athens.[17] It would not be strange, then, if Plato should make special provision for punishing this kind of slave-murder. Elsewhere, in connection with the law punishing neglect of parents, Plato lays it upon the magistrates to secure the slave who gives information of such neglect against injury at the hands of those against whom he has informed (XI, 932d).

A question arises as to the procedure used in punishing offenses against this law. Plato prescribes that the offender shall be liable to a *δίκη φόνου*. But the prosecution of murder, both in Platonic and in Attic law, rested with the relatives of the victim. Who then is to avenge the murder of the slave? It is reasonable to suppose that Plato is taking for granted a provision of Attic law that gave the master the right to prosecute for the murder of his slave.[18] But what if it is the master who has murdered his own slave for fear that he will give information? Here again a possible answer is provided by Attic law, which permitted another member of the family to bring

---

[16] Below, p. 76.

[17] Antiphon V, 52: "If I had had anything to conceal," says the accused, "I would have put these men out of the way when it was in my power, and not have left them alive as informers (*μηνυταί*) against me." Cf. Lysias VII, 16.

[18] Dem. XLVII, 72, with which Pollux VIII, 118 is almost verbally identical. Cf. also Antiphon V, 48: *εἴπερ γὰρ . . . ἔξεστι . . . τῷ δεσπότῃ, ἂν δοκῇ, ἐπεξελθεῖν ὑπὲρ τοῦ δούλου κτλ.*

suit against the murderer of the slave.[19] It might seem that with such a procedure the chances of bringing a murderer to justice are very small; but Plato elsewhere provides that a failure to prosecute for murder makes the delinquent individual liable to prosecution for impiety by any qualified citizen (IX, 868abd, 871b). A similar provision existed in Attic law,[20] permitting the γραφὴ ἀσεβείας to be brought against a kinsman who failed to prosecute. By this device did Attic law (and Plato's law likewise) reconcile the principle that murder was a private wrong with the interest of the community in avoiding the pollution of unpunished murder.

The interpretation we have given to the law of 872c has the result of leaving a gap in Plato's law of homicide, in that there is no provision covering the deliberate murder of a slave not an informer. Purification would be required, of course, and compensation to the owner if the victim belonged to some one other than the slayer: this much we may infer from the previous laws. Whether any other penalty would be imposed we cannot say. Attic law, as we have already said, permitted the master in such cases to bring a δίκη φόνου against the murderer; or, if the murderer was the master, allowed another member of the same family to bring suit. In such cases the trial came before one of the ancient homicide courts, the Palladium, which also tried cases involving the murder of *metics*. The penalty imposed by this court seems to have been exile.[21]

Not only does Plato's law fail to prescribe penalties or procedures to protect the life of the slave, but it denies the slave the right to protect himself against a murderous assault. The slave who kills a freeman in self-defense is to be put to death unless he is pardoned by his victim before he expires, though a freeman who kills another in defending himself has committed only justifiable homicide (IX, 869d). Elsewhere the law prescribes that a person committing rape on a *free* woman can be put to death with impunity, either by the woman her-

---

[19] Plato *Euthyphro*, 4b-d, seems to show that this procedure, though unusual, was in accordance with law. Kin-slaying was certainly an offense actionable at Attic law (Treston, *Poine*, pp. 237, 253 ff.), and the slave, as respects the law of homicide, is treated as a member of the family. For a fuller discussion of the *Euthyphro* see the author's article in *Class. Phil.* XXXII (1937), 220 ff.

[20] Bonner and Smith, II, 213 f., Dem. XXII, 2, and *Class. Phil.* XXXII (1937), 219.

[21] Aristotle, *Const. of Athens* LVII, 3; Isocrates XVIII, 52; Dem. XLVII, 69, 70; Aeschines Schol. II, 87, and *Class. Phil.* XXXII (1937), 213. The γραφὴ ὕβρεως could of course also be used to prosecute the deliberate murder of a slave. No doubt the "many Athenians" who, Demosthenes says, had paid the penalty of death for *hybris* against slaves were guilty of murder.

self or by her relatives (IX, 874c). Evidently a similar assault upon a slave-woman could not be met by such a summary remedy. Whether the slave had the right of self-defense in Attic law is not known, though a statement in Plato's *Gorgias*, if taken at its face value, would indicate that he had no such right.[22]

Plato makes no mention of a right of asylum for slaves. Attic custom permitted a slave to escape from a cruel master by taking refuge in the Theseum or at the altar of the Eumenides on the Areopagus, and there demand to be sold to another master. There seems to have been no legal means whereby such a demand could be enforced, but if the priest of the sanctuary granted asylum, there was no way open to the master to regain possession, and thus he would probably be compelled to sell his slave as the best way out of a bad situation.[23] Plato's failure to mention a right of asylum is the more marked in that he deals at some length with the procedure for regaining possession of a runaway slave.[24]

Thus we see that Plato's law recognizes the person of the slave as worthy of protection, both in the doctrine that the shedding of slave-blood involves pollution, and in the injunction to avoid *hybris* in the treatment of slaves. In these respects Plato is following ancient and hallowed principles of Attic law, and of Greek law generally. The slave, from this point of view, is not merely a piece of property, an animated tool, but a member of the religious community; and the power of a master over his slave is not an absolute power of life and death, but is limited by what is "holy." Now in Attic law we know that these principles had the support also of the state and its courts, so that a violation of them would expose a man to civil as well as religious penalties. But although Plato's law gives the slave a right to trial (in at least some cases) and thus seems to imply that the life of a slave cannot lawfully be taken without judicial process, yet in only one case (the murder of a slave informer) is there any mention of the *δίκη φόνου* being used against the slayer, or any mention of civil penalties (apart from the payment of damages to the slave's owner and a penalty in some cases for litigation) incurred by the slayer. Nor are there any methods of self-help that a slave may lawfully employ. Shall we give Plato the benefit of the doubt and assume

[22] *Gorgias* 483b: ἀνδραπόδου . . . ὅστις ἀδικούμενος καὶ προπηλακιζόμενος μὴ οἷός τέ ἐστιν αὐτὸς αὑτῷ βοηθεῖν μηδὲ ἄλλῳ οὗ ἂν κήδηται.

[23] On the right of asylum in Attic law see Beauchet, II, 438, Westermann, p. 921. Such a right was recognized also at Andania (*Sylloge*, No. 736, lines 81 ff.) and in the law of Gortyn (Col. I, line 39, Bücheler-Zitelmann, p. 18).

[24] See below, p. 111.

that he intended to take over the usual procedures and penalties of Attic law with respect to slave-homicide? Or shall we assume that he proposed to put the slave more fully under the dominion of the master than he was under Attic law, and hold the master responsible in the main only to his conscience and to the precepts of religion?

In only one point does Plato's law clearly rise above the law of Athens, and that is in the protection it gives the slave informer. Attic law, so far as we know, punished the killing of an informer like the killing of any other slave, viz. with exile.[25] It is indicative of the spirit of Plato's reforms that when his law does give special protection to the slave it is to protect him as a possible *μηνυτής*, that is, as an instrument, though a humble one, in the enforcement of the laws.

[25] Of course if the slayer of a slave-informer were proceeded against by the *γραφὴ ὕβρεως*, the penalty could be death.

Chapter IV

THE OFFENSES OF SLAVES

For breaches of household discipline the slave is liable, of course, only to his master. In this chapter we shall be concerned with offenses committed by the slave against persons other than his master, i.e. offenses against the law of the city. Plato's law under this head is by no means complete; nevertheless the provisions that it contains enable us to formulate a fairly satisfactory conception of the main principles involved. The unlawful acts mentioned may conveniently be divided into four classes: (a) offenses against property; (b) *αἰκία*, i.e. assault without bodily injury, and *τραῦμα*, bodily injury; (c) homicide; and (d) offenses against the public. I shall first cite the legislation covering these offenses and then comment upon the principles involved.

(a) The law covering damage to property by slaves is identical in principle with that which applies when damage has been done by a beast of burden or any other domestic animal (XI, 936e).

> If a slave man or woman damages anything belonging to another, and the person who suffers the damage is in no wise a contributory cause through his inexperience or general ignorance, the master of the slave who has done the harm shall make good the loss in full, or give up the offending slave (XI 936cd; cf. VIII, 846a).

So much for the underlying principle. But it is assumed that for trifling offenses against property the injured person will ordinarily get satisfaction by flogging the slave. The following law is typical:

> If a slave takes anything of this sort [i.e. fruit] without the consent of the owner of the land, he shall be whipped with as many strokes as the number of grapes or figs that he has taken (VIII, 845a).

For such offenses punishment would ordinarily be inflicted immediately by the owner or his agent. Likewise a slave who attempts to appropriate an article left behind by its owner is to be whipped. Since in such cases the owner would not be present, the punishment is to be inflicted by anyone over thirty years of age who happens to be at hand (XI, 914b). It is probable that in all such cases the master would have the right to pay for the damage and deal with his slave himself as he saw fit, as is prescribed in the more general law of XI, 936e.

(b) Τραῦμα and αἰκία.

If a slave wounds (τρώσῃ) a freeman in a fit of anger, the master shall deliver the slave to the injured person, who may do with him what he will (χρῆσθαι ὅτι ἂν ἐθέλῃ). If the master does not surrender the slave, he shall himself make full amends for the injury (IX, 879a).

If a slave strikes a freeman, whether citizen or foreigner, everyone near by shall come to the victim's assistance, or else pay the fine which has been specified (cf. 880b). And they shall help bind the aggressor and shall deliver him to the injured person. And he shall take and bind him and flog him as he pleases (μαστιγώσας ὁπόσας ἂν ἐθέλῃ), but without injuring the master (μηδὲν βλάπτων τὸν δεσπότην), and then shall deliver him to his lawful owner. . . . The master shall receive him from the injured person and shall not free him from his bonds until the slave persuades the man he has struck that he deserves to be set free (IX, 882ab).

(c) For killing a freeman in self-defense the slave is to be put to death, unless before the victim dies he absolves the slave of guilt (IX, 869d; cf. 869a). For killing a freeman in anger the slave is to be delivered to the relatives of the dead man, who are required to put him to death, the manner of execution, however, being left to their discretion (IX, 868c). If the slave has killed his own master in a fit of anger, the dead man's relatives are likewise to punish the slave as they will, but they must under no circumstances allow him to live (IX, 868b). For willful murder the slave is to be taken by the public executioner to the grave of his victim, where he is to be flogged to the satisfaction of the dead man's avenger (ὁ ἑλών, the prosecutor who has won the case against him) and then, "if he survives the beating (ἐάνπερ βιῷ παιόμενος)," he is to be put to death (IX, 872b).

No mention is made of the penalty for bodily injuries inflicted by one slave upon another. Presumably this would be regarded as damage to property, for which the master of the injured slave could obtain satisfaction from the master of the aggressor. But a slave who willfully kills another slave is to be put to death (IX, 872ab), though if he kills in self-defense he is required only to undergo ceremonial purification for the shedding of blood (IX, 869d).

(d) For temple-robbing the slave is to be branded on hands and forehead, beaten with as many stripes as the judges think fit, and driven naked across the borders of the land (IX, 854d). When a slave has stolen public property the court may fix the penalty as it sees fit, but the judges are to remember that such an offender is probably curable, i.e. neither death nor exile would ordinarily be imposed (XII, 941d). Among offenses against the public may be classed the failure of a slave to give *μήνυσις*, i.e. to lay information before a magistrate regarding a breach of the law. If a slave knows of some one who has appropriated buried treasure and fails to inform the magistrates he is to be put to death (XI, 914a). The same penalty is probably intended when a slave fails to give *μήνυσις* regarding neglect of parents (XI, 932d), for in this, as in the preceding case, the reward of freedom follows the giving of *μήνυσις*. Again Platonic law lays upon the slave the obligation to come to the aid of a parent when attacked by his child, and failure to do this carries the penalty of a hundred stripes (IX, 881c).

There are four points involved in this legislation that can best be treated separately: (1) the nature and extent of the master's liability for the unlawful acts of his slaves; (2) the master's right to protect his slave from punishment by compounding for the injury; (3) the nature of the punishments prescribed for slaves; and (4) the recognition of the slave's personality before the law of the city.

(1) The principle that the master is responsible for the acts of his slaves is clearly stated in the above laws covering property damage and bodily injury. It is a principle that was generally recognized in Greek as well as in Roman law,[1] and had its source no doubt, as Glotz maintains,[2] in the solidarity of the family, whereby in more primitive times the family was collectively liable for the injuries caused by any one of its members. The slave was regarded as a member of the family in Greek law, and since the master was the head of the family, it is he who necessarily assumed liability for the actions of the slave. In the same way the head of the family was liable for the acts of his wife and children, though in classical times this liability under Greek law seems to have been limited, in the case of sons, to the minority of the child. The slave was looked upon

[1] Hyperides cites and ascribes to Solon the following law: *τὰς ζημίας ἃς ἂν ἐργάσωνται οἱ οἰκέται καὶ τὰ ἀδικήματα διαλύειν τὸν δεσπότην παρ' ᾧ ἂν ἐργάσωνται οἱ οἰκέται* (*Athenog.* 22, c. 10) For Attic law see also Lysias X, 19. This is a textually defective passage, but as interpreted by the editors of *Dikaiomata* (p. 111) reads as follows: *οἰκῆος καὶ δούλης διπλῆν τὴν βλάβην ὀφείλειν*, the genitives *οἰκῆος* and *δούλης* being genitives of the agent. According to this law, then, the master is responsible for injuries done by his slaves and pays double. The law of Gortyn held a master responsible, both for his *κατακείμενοι*, i.e. men of free birth bound to him for debt, and for his *δοῦλοι* (Kohler-Ziebarth, pp. 31, 34, 53, 54). The master's responsibility is also asserted in the law of the *Lille Papyrus*, representing third-century law, probably of the city of Naucratis (Kohler-Ziebarth, pp. 104–105); in the *Papyrus Halensis*, which gives us Alexandrian law of the third century (Meyer, pp. 241 f., *Dikaiomata*, pp. 22, 107); in a third-century inscription from Mylasa in Asia Minor (*OG.*, No. 515); in an inscription from the island of Syros (*Sylloge* (2nd ed.), No. 680); and in a first-century inscription from Andania in the Peloponnesus (*Sylloge*, No. 736).

[2] Glotz, *La solidarité de la famille*, pp. 165 ff.

as a permanently "minor" (i.e. legally immature) member of the family; hence the liability of the slave's master lasted as long as his ownership of the slave.

Of particular interest is the way in which a master is permitted to discharge his liability, i.e. he may either pay for the damage caused or surrender his slave to the injured person (IX, 879a; XI, 936cd). In no case is he held liable in his own person, if the slave has acted without his knowledge. This point is clearly brought out in the law of IX, 882b, where a person who has been attacked by a slave is explicitly forbidden to take vengeance upon the master (*μηδὲν βλάπτων τὸν δεσπότην*) though he may bind and flog the slave to his heart's content. If the injury done is too great to be atoned for by the flogging of the slave, the injured party may demand compensation, whereupon the master has the alternative of paying for the injury or surrendering the slave. The latter is the familiar *noxae datio* of Roman law, i.e. the gift of the *noxa*, or offending object, to the injured party.[3] With the delivery of the offending slave the master is quit of all further liability, but the slave becomes the property of the person who has been injured. This seems also to have been the general procedure of Greek law, so far as we can determine.[4] The *noxae datio* is clearly provided in the law of the *Lille Papyrus*.[5] And something very much like it appears in the inscription from Andania, which permits the master to deliver the slave to the injured party to work out the equivalent of the damage caused.[6] This is not identical with the *noxae datio*, for the ownership of the slave is not transferred, though if the damage was great enough that would logically follow. We have no conclusive evidence that the *noxae datio* was permitted in Attic law for the offenses of slaves; though a passage from Bekker's *Anecdota* suggests it,[7] and Beauchet plausibly argues that since the *noxae datio* is known to have been permitted in the case of offending animals, it must likewise have been permitted when the injury was caused by slaves.[8] We may also argue from the recognition of the *noxae datio* by the *Lille Papyrus*, for the law of this fragment shows many other similarities to Attic law. Furthermore, there is nothing in any of the fragments of Attic

[3] *Institutes*, IV, vii, 1–20; *Digest* IX, iv, 1. For the *noxae datio* among the Germans, Norwegians, Slavs, and Hungarians, see Glotz, p. 177, n.2.

[4] Partsch, *Archiv*, VI, 65–74; Glotz, pp. 177 f.

[5] Col. II, lines 26 ff. (Meyer, p. 246).

[6] *Sylloge*, No. 736, lines 77 ff.

[7] Bekker, *Anecdota*, I, 187: *ἐγγυῆσαι: ὅταν τις κρινόμενος παράσχῃ δοῦλον ἀνθ' ἑαυτοῦ τιμωρηθῆναι.*

[8] Beauchet, II, 456; and Xen. *Hell.* II, 4, 41.

slave-law that have come down to us to suggest that the liability of the master extends beyond what he can discharge by the delivery of the slave to the injured party, and this is the most important effect of the *noxae datio*.

In both the cases in which the *noxae datio* is explicitly provided for by Platonic law, there are additional prescriptions protecting a master against fraud in a suit arising out of injuries done by his slave. The law above quoted concerning property damage done by a slave continues as follows:

> If the master claims that there has been collusion between the injured party and his slave for the purpose of depriving him of ownership of the slave, let him bring an accusation of fraud (κακοτεχνιῶν) against him who claims to have been injured (τῷ φάσκοντι βλαβῆναι). If he wins the suit, he shall receive double the value of the slave as estimated by the court; if he loses, he shall pay the damages claimed and surrender the slave besides (XI, 936de).

The remedy of the δίκη κακοτεχνιῶν which this law provides is one that existed in Attic law. From the grammarians and the orators we learn that it was a suit brought against a person guilty of adducing false evidence in the courts, and therefore was closely connected with the suit for perjury (the δίκη ψευδομαρτυριῶν).[9] The connection between these two suits seems to be as follows. The δίκη ψευδομαρτυριῶν was directed at the witness, whereas the δίκη κακοτεχνιῶν was directed at the principal, and would not lie unless a previous δίκη ψευδομαρτυριῶν had been successful. Both suits were subsidiary to the original suit at which the evidence questioned was introduced.[10] Now the Platonic law above quoted fits very nicely into this picture of Attic law. The text indicates that the fact of injury sustained is open to question (cf. τῷ φάσκοντι βλαβῆναι), so that the issue really hinges upon the validity of the evidence adduced to support the legal claim to damages. But Plato's law here makes no mention of a previous suit for perjury, though the δίκη ψευδομαρτυριῶν appears elsewhere in Platonic law (XI, 937b ff.). The reason for its absence here seems clear. Collusion between the plaintiff and the defendant's slave has been alleged, and such collusion, one may infer, would consist in the bringing of false evidence

---

[9] Bekker, *Anecdota*, I, 268, 24; Pollux VIII, 37. The grammarians are confirmed by Dem. XLVII, 1; XLIX, 56.

[10] Rentsch, *De δίκη ψευδομαρτυριῶν in jure attico comparatis Platonis imprimis legum libris cum oratoribus atticis*, pp. 55 ff.; Dem. XLVII, 1; XLIX, 56, Schol. in *Leges*, 936d (Ruhnke, p. 241).

to support the plaintiff's claim to damages. Now if the slave's own statements were submitted in evidence, they could not be attacked by the *δίκη ψευδομαρτυριῶν*; for according to Attic law a slave's testimony, if given in court, would take the form of questioning under torture, and such *βάσανοι*, as they were called, were not subject to legal attack.[11] If, on the other hand, the slave's statement was submitted by the claimant before bringing suit, in order to obtain a settlement out of court (and such settlements out of court were encouraged by Platonic law, as is shown by the numerous penalties for litigation that occur),[12] in this case also a *δίκη ψευδομαρτυριῶν* would not lie, for such a suit applied only to judicially submitted evidence. This explains why the *δίκη ψευδομαρτυριῶν* does not appear in the Platonic law we are now examining. The *δίκη κακοτεχνιῶν* would, if successful, have the double effect of setting aside the judgment in the original suit (when an actual suit for damages had been brought) and of securing satisfaction to the defendant in that suit for the damages caused by the plaintiff's fradulent prosecution. Whether it was a departure from Attic law to permit the *δίκη κακοτεχνιῶν* in these circumstances without a previous *δίκη ψευδομαρτυριῶν* we cannot say; but in any case it is clear that Plato is thinking of *κακοτεχνιῶν* in its strict Attic sense as an attempt to establish a legal contention by false evidence, and not in the more general sense of deceit or fraud.[13]

The law of *τραῦμα* provides a somewhat different remedy for the protection of the master against unfounded claims.

> If he (the master) claims that the suit is a trick agreed upon between the slave and the man who has been assaulted, let him contest the matter in court. If he loses, he shall pay triple compensation for the injury, and if he wins, the person who has connived with the slave shall be liable for man-stealing (ἀνδραποδισμοῦ) (IX, 879a).

Here the *δίκη κακοτεχνιῶν* does not appear; its place is taken by a suit for man-stealing. Besides the difference in procedure, there appears to be a difference in the penalties prescribed. Man-stealing was a very grave crime at Athens, punished in some periods at least (perhaps in all) by death;[14] and although Plato's law does not name

[11] See below, p. 81. [12] See above, p. 52.

[13] Hence the view of Rentsch (*op. cit.* pp. 55 f.) and Thalheim (in Pauly-Wissowa, *s.v.* *κακοτεχνίαι*) that Plato gives the *δίκη κακοτεχνιῶν* a more general application than it had in Attic law would seem to be an error.

[14] Lycurgus (Fr. 62, Blass) says that the ἀνδραποδιστής was punished with death at Athens, and by ἀνδραποδιστής he means one who steals slaves (see the Budé edition of Lycurgus,

the penalty, it must have been more severe than the "double damages" prescribed by the law of XI, 936de. On the surface it would seem that the two cases of collusion are essentially similar, differing only in the fact that in the one case it is property damage and in the other case personal injury which is falsely alleged, the intent in both cases being the same, viz. to gain possession of the slave. There seems then no material difference capable of explaining the difference in procedure; and one suspects that we have here two separate proposals for dealing with a situation not clearly covered by Attic law.[15]

The discharge of liability by the *noxae datio* is permitted, in the Greek codes, only when the slave has acted without the knowledge or consent of his master. If he has acted under the direction of his master, or if his master, though not ordering the action, knew of it and took no steps to prevent it, the master also is held liable, as in Roman law.[16] The laws of Gortyn provide that the slave (in this case the law refers to the κατακείμενος, or debt-slave) who, at the command of his master, uses another's land or carries away another's crops shall go unpunished; only the master is liable.[17] The *Lille Papyrus* seems to follow the same principle: if a slave has committed a wrong and the court decides that the master has ordered, or at least known of the slave's action, the damages shall be assessed against the master; nothing is said about punishing the slave.[18] But a second-century inscription from Pergamum provides that when the slave has acted with his master's knowledge both master and slave shall be punished.[19] Perhaps the inscription from Syros prescribing penalties for both master and slave when the slave has violated the law refers to this type of offense.[20] Attic law distinguished between the unlawful act of a slave who was carrying out his master's orders and an offense committed on his own initiative, and provided that in the latter case the suit should be directed against the slave, not the master.[21] There is nothing in Platonic law

p. 94). Cf. Xen. *Apol.* 25. The ἀνδραποδιστής belonged to the class of miscreants (κακοῦργοι) who were *ipso facto* deprived of the ordinary guarantees of personal freedom, i.e., they were subject to summary arrest (ἀπαγωγή) by the injured party. Vinogradoff, *Historical Jurisprudence*, II, 186, 190; Lipsius, pp. 319 f.

[15] There are a few other such inconsistencies in the *Laws*. Compare, for example, the punishment for theft of public property in XII, 942a with that prescribed in IX, 857b.

[16] Ulpian, in the *Digest*, IX, iv, 2.

[17] Kohler-Ziebarth, pp. 30–31.

[18] Col. II, lines 17 ff. (Meyer, p. 246).

[19] *OG.* No. 483, lines 715 ff.

[20] *Sylloge* (2nd ed.), No. 680.

[21] Dem. LV, 31, 32, 34; XXXVII, 51; Lipsius, p. 795: Beauchet, II, 458–459.

applying to the former type of case; the provisions we have cited obviously refer to delicts committed by the slave on his own initiative. That Plato would permit a master who had instigated his slave to a wrongful act to escape liability by merely surrendering his slave to the injured party is unthinkable, and without parallel, so far as we know, in either Greek or Roman law.[22]

It is to be noted that the *noxae datio* is not mentioned in the law of VIII, 845a, covering petty thievery, nor in the law of *αἰκία* (IX, 880b). In these cases the master's liability is discharged by his allowing the slave to be whipped by the injured party; but the slave remains his property and is restored to him after the punishment has been inflicted. The law of *αἰκία* has its parallel in the law of Alexandria which likewise makes no mention of the *noxae datio* but provides flogging for certain offenses (such as threatening with a dangerous weapon, or actual assault) committed by slaves upon free persons. The master however must pay damages for the injury if he refuses to let his slave be flogged.[23] Likewise the provisions of the *Digest* concerning *injuriae* committed by slaves allow the master to deliver his slave for flogging (*verberandum exhibere*) and regard this as satisfying the injured person's claim.[24] Here we have a type of surrender falling short of the *noxae datio* but quite similar in principle. The absence of the *noxae datio* in these laws does not mean that a different principle is applied in cases of *αἰκία*, but only that the damages claimed in compensation for this type of injury would ordinarily not come to the value of the slave, hence the master would have no reason for invoking the privilege of the *noxae datio*.[25]

---

[22] Partsch, *Archiv*, VI, 73. Unless we take Bekker, *Anecdota* I, 187 (cited above, p. 60n) as referring to cases of this sort; but more probably it refers to cases in which the master has been adjudged liable for acts of his slaves done without his knowledge.

[23] *Papyrus Halensis*, lines 188 ff. (*Dikaiomata*, p. 107): *ἐὰν δὲ ὁ δ[οῦλος ἢ ἡ] δούλη τούτων τι ποιήσῃ τῷ ἐλευθέρῳ ἢ τῇ ἐλευθέ[ρᾳ μασ]τιγούσθω μὴ ἔλασσον [ἑκατὸν] πληγῶν ἢ τὴν ζημίαν διπλασία[ν ἀπο]τεισάτω ὁ δεσπότης τοῦ ποιήσαντος [τ]ῷ παθόντι.* Cf. also lines 197 ff. Partsch, *Archiv*, VI, 68, ascribes a similar principle to Attic law.

[24] *In arbitrio domini est, an velit eum* [i.e. *servum*] *verberandum exhibere, ut ita satisfiat ei qui injuriam passus est*, XLVII, 10, 17, 4. On the possibility that Roman law on this point was influenced by the law of Alexandria, see Visscher, "Le délit d'injuria commis par un esclave," in *Rev. Hist. de Droit Français*, IX (1930), 606–608.

[25] In the same way the differences between the *Papyrus Halensis* and the *Lille Papyrus* can be explained without assuming (with the editors of *Dikaiomata*, p. 112) that they represent divergent principles. The failure of the *Papyrus Halensis* to mention the *noxae datio* in connection with *αἰκία* does not mean that the law of Alexandria did not recognize it in connection with graver personal injuries and property damages. The law of the *Lille Papyrus* deals with *ἀδικήματα* in general, and therefore states the more general procedure of the *noxae datio*. Cf. Partsch, *Archiv*, VI, 66. One suspects that the commentators have been misled by a too

(2) But the surrender of the slave is not obligatory upon the master, at least for the first two classes of offenses. In XI, 936cd and 879a, it is explicitly provided that the master may, if he pleases, pay for the injury caused, i.e. he may buy off the vengeance of the aggrieved person. In the law of *αἰκία* the alternative of paying damages is not mentioned, but it is clearly implied. The situation envisaged in the text is one in which the injured person is able to inflict immediate punishment on the slave. If the slave, however, gets away and the master refuses to surrender him for punishment, the injured party must perforce be satisfied with the payment of damages. Furthermore, when the slave is guilty of *τραῦμα* Plato permits the master to pay for the injury, and *τραῦμα* is clearly the graver offense, involving all the indignity of *αἰκία* plus the physical hurt. We can only think then that for *αἰκία* as well as for *τραῦμα* Plato would permit the master to free his slave from punishment by paying for the injury. Thus this law falls into agreement with the preceding ones.

If this is the correct interpretation of Plato's law, it accords also with the general practice of both Greek and Roman law with respect to an indignity (*αἰκία*, *ὕβρις*, *injuria*) suffered by a freeman at the hand of a slave. We have just seen that the *Papyrus Halensis* gives the master the right to protect his slave from punishment by paying a fine.[26] That this fine is in some cases double and in some cases triple the fine imposed for the same offense when committed by a free man merely indicates that the injury to be compensated for is a graver one.[27] The same right is given the master in the inscriptions from Andania, Mylasa, and Syros, though in the inscription from Pergamum such a right is not mentioned. Roman law gave the master the alternative of delivering the slave to be whipped (*verberandum exhibere*) or compounding for the injury (*litis aestimatio*).[28]

literal attention to the three alternatives given in the Digest (XLVII, 10, 17, 4): *dabitur ei* [i.e. *domino*] *facultas praestare ei servum verberandum aut, si de eo verberibus satis non fiat, noxae dedendum vel litis aestimationem sufferendam.* It is clear that this does not cover all the alternatives permitted in Greek law, for the sacral statute of Andania provides that the master may surrender his slave to work out the damage caused (see p. 60, n. 6). It would seem simpler to say that Greek law recognized only two genuine alternatives: the payment of damages by the master, and the surrender of the offending slave. This surrender, in turn, might be the full transfer of ownership effected by the *noxae datio*, or a temporary surrender for punishment or for working out the damage caused.

[26] See above, note 23.

[27] See below, note 45. The master pays double if he wishes to avoid the flogging of his slave, and triple if he contests the case in court. Thus there is a penalty for litigation also involved.

[28] Ulpian, in the *Digest*, XLVII, 10, 17, 4 (cited above, note 25).

But when the slave is guilty of homicide the master has no alternative but to surrender him for punishment. This is in accordance with the principle that there can be no composition for bloodshed. The shedding of blood involves pollution that must be wiped out either by the offender's blood or (for lesser degrees of homicide) by a ceremonial purification.[29] When a slave kills a freeman only the slave's blood will atone for the offense. It would seem that at least when the slave is acting on his own initiative the master is in no wise held responsible beyond the obligation to surrender his slave to justice, but this he must do.

For offenses against the public it would also seem that the master has no option, but must surrender his slave for punishment. No mention is made of the master's right to compound for these offenses, and their nature is such that composition could hardly have been permitted. For both temple-robbing and theft of public property the penalty, when the offender is a citizen, is death (IX, 854e; XII, 942a).[30] Similar reasoning applies to the failure to denounce and the failure to come to the aid of a stricken parent. A freeman guilty of these same crimes of omission is punished in the former case with dishonor, and in the latter case with cursing (XI, 914a, IX, 881d). In other words, these are not venial offenses. We can scarcely go wrong, then, in concluding that for these and all other offenses against the public the penalty must be exacted from the slave's person. But, as in the case of homicide, when the slave has acted on his own initiative the master's liability apparently extends no further than the delivery of his slave for punishment.

(3) Let us now consider the punishment inflicted on the slave. The first point to note is the frequent use of the whip. Plato has earlier laid down the principle that slaves are to be chastised, free men admonished (VI, 777e).[31] In accordance with this principle we find that flogging is the usual penalty for offenses committed by slaves. The freeman may be fined, imprisoned, disgraced, deprived of civic rights, exiled, put to death, but only in the rarest cases and for the gravest offenses is he subjected to the indignity of the whip.[32]

---

[29] See above, p. 50.

[30] Yet IX, 857b seems to impose only the penalty of double restitution for theft of public property. If it is correct to interpret the passage thus, then there is a clear inconsistency in Plato's legislation. There can be no doubt that 942a is more in accord with the spirit of his legislation. Perhaps 857b expresses Attic law.

[31] See above, p. 44.

[32] There are five places in the *Laws* where flogging is prescribed for citizens: VI, 762c, for the ἀγρονόμος who neglects his duty; XI, 932b, for the child or person under thirty who

Of particular interest is the law forbidding the picking of fruit destined for storage. If a foreigner and his slave through ignorance of this law pick some of the forbidden fruit, the freeman is to be told of the law and warned against future violations; the slave, however, is to be whipped (VIII, 845a).

This sharp distinction between flogging and punishments suitable for freemen is found in all the Greek codes that have come down to us. Demosthenes, probably expressing not only an Athenian but a common Greek rule of law, says that the chief distinction between slaves and freemen is that for unlawful acts the former are punished in their bodies, the latter in their property.[33] This principle is amply borne out by the inscriptions and papyri. The sacral statute of Andania (first century B.C.) provides that for theft committed during a religious festival the freeman is to be fined twice the worth of the article, the slave is to be flogged and fined twice the worth of the article.[34] For cutting wood in the sacred enclosure the slave is to be whipped, the freeman fined. For violating the ordinances respecting buying and selling, the slave is to be whipped, the freeman fined twenty drachmae; likewise for violating the ordinances respecting the water supply. An inscription from Delphi (96 B.C.) prescribes that for offenses within the sacred enclosure the slave is to be flogged by the officers, the freeman to be fined two hundred silver drachmae.[35] Similarly an inscription from Pergamum (second century B.C.) prescribes that the slave who pollutes a public well (if he has acted without his master's knowledge) shall lose his possessions (ὧν μὲν ἂν ἔχῃ στερέσθω), shall be given a hundred stripes, be put in prison for ten days, and when he comes forth he is to be flogged again, this time not less than fifty stripes. For the same offense the freeman is to lose the vessel or clothing he has brought to the well and be fined fifty drachmae.[36] Likewise at Mylasa (third century B.C.) for violating the banking ordinances the freeman is to be fined, the slave to be punished with fifty stripes and six months imprisonment.[37] Again

---

neglects his parents; IX, 881d, and VI, 784d, for the person who has become ἄτιμος and who fails to abide by the ἀτιμία; and lastly, the curious case of VIII, 845c, reminiscent of Sparta, which prescribes flogging for a citizen under thirty who is *caught* stealing fruit. It is distinctly said that if he evades detection there is no shame attached to the act. It will be noted that in three of the cases the citizen is under thirty years of age, in the other two he is already ἄτιμος, therefore not in full possession of the rights of citizenship. It would seem therefore that the citizen of mature age and in good repute was not subject to this species of penalty.

[33] Dem. XXII, 55. Cf. also XXIV, 167, in part identical; and Aristoph. *Clouds* 1413–1414.

[34] *Sylloge*, No. 736, lines 75, 80, 103, 106, 111.

[35] *Sylloge*, No. 729, lines 6 ff.

[36] *OG.* No. 483, lines 168–184.

[37] *OG.*, No. 515, lines 29 ff.

at Syros for violating the ordinances respecting the conduct of the torch races, the slave is to be given one hundred stripes, the freeman is to be fined one hundred fifty drachmae.[38] A multilated fourth-century inscription from Athens testifies eloquently to the distinction in status between freeman and slave.[39] Aeschines refers to a law prescribing fifty stripes which is attributed to Solon.[40] Another Attic inscription of the late fourth century provides that for cutting wood in the sacred precincts of Apollo Erithaseus the priest shall administer fifty stripes, if the offender is a slave, and impose a fine of fifty drachmae if the offender is a freeman.[41]

Glotz, from an analysis of these and other inscriptions, concludes that the penal law of Athens was much more humane than that of other Greek cities, in that (1) the number of stripes to be received by the slave was equal to the number of drachmae to be paid by the freeman (a drachma was the ordinary day's wage in the fifth century); (2) the legal number of stripes prescribed was a maximum and the punishment was always to be proportioned to the offense; and (3) public functionaries, not having the right to fix a fine of more than fifty drachmae without appeal had also no right to inflict more than fifty stripes.[42] There is no doubt that as compared, for example, with the severity of the inscription from Pergamum the inscriptions from Attica make a most favorable impression. If Glotz's view is correct, the Platonic law is distinctly severer than Attic law. Sometimes the number of stripes to be inflicted is not specified (*μαστιγωθεὶς ὁπόσας ἂν δόξῃ τοῖς δικασταῖς*, IX, 854d; *μαστιγώσας ὁπόσας ἂν ἐθέλῃ*, IX, 882b; *πολλὰς πληγάς*, XI, 914b, where the determination of the number is left to the person administering the penalty). And where the number is specified it seems out of all accord with the Athenian principle of one stripe to one drachma. Thus for picking fruit without permission the slave receives a stripe for every grape or fig he has taken (VIII, 845a). Since Platonic law punishes theft by a freeman with the penalty of double restitution (IX, 857a), we get the result that one stripe for the slave equals two figs for the freeman. The penalty of a hundred stripes to be inflicted by the magistrates

---

[38] *Sylloge* (2nd ed.), No. 680, lines 1 ff. Cf. also No. 1217, lines 6 ff. (Thasos).

[39] *Sylloge*, No. 313, line 40: ἐὰμ μ[ὲν δοῦλος ἦι . . . λ]αμ[βαν]έτω . . . πλ[ηγάς . . . ἐὰν] δ'[ἐλε]ύθερ[ος. . . .

[40] *Timarchus* 8, 139.

[41] *Sylloge*, No. 984, lines 8 ff. Cf. also the frequent use of the stick upon slaves in Attic comedy. Aristoph. *Wasps*, 1307; *Frogs*, 812–813. Pollux III, 78–79 enumerates several different instruments used in punishing slaves, some of them clearly types of whips or scourges.

[42] "Les esclaves et la peine du fouet," in *Comptes-Rendues de l'Académie des Inscriptions et Belles-Lettres*, 1908, pp. 571–586.

on a slave who fails to assist a parent who is attacked by his child is just double that which, according to Glotz, Attic law permitted the magistrates to inflict without court authorization (IX, 881c). Again we are told by the Old Oligarch that at Athens it was forbidden to strike a slave (i.e. obviously a slave not one's own);[43] and we hear of private suits arising from the slander of a freeman by a slave.[44] All this suggests that Attic law did not permit a person injured by a slave not his own to take summary action against the offender; whereas this, as we have seen, is a fairly common feature of Plato's law.

Especially severe are the penalties Plato prescribes for offenses against the person of freemen. For *αἰκία*, as we have seen, the law permits the offended person to bind the slave and whip him as much as he pleases. When the slave has inflicted a wound, the wounded man may punish him as he pleases. Although Plato recognizes degrees of homicide when committed by slaves, yet in all cases the penalty is death, except when, after killing in self-defense, the slave secures the pardon of his victim before he expires. This uniform penalty of death is the more striking when we note that if a freeman kills in self-defense it counts as justifiable homicide and carries only the penalty of ritual purification for the pollution of shedding blood (IX, 869d). And when a freeman kills another in anger the punishment is exile for two, or in some cases three years (IX, 866d, 867cd). Again, when one slave kills another in self-defense, ritual purification of the slayer is all that is required (IX, 869d). The principle underlying this part of Plato's legislation is not hard to find: the gravity of an injury is determined, not merely by the harm resulting, but also by the status of the person who causes it. Since the slave occupies an inferior position, an injury brought about by a slave is much more serious than the same injury caused by a freeman.[45]

[43] [Xen.] *Const. of Athens.* I, 10. Cf. also the *Lille Papyrus* (Col. I, lines 13–15; Meyer, pp. 245–246) where it is forbidden to brand or flog (?) a slave without authorization (the text is mutilated and it cannot be determined what sort of authorization is required).

[44] Arist. *Const. of Athens*, LIX, 5; Pollux, VIII, 88.

[45] Cf. Ulpian, in the *Digest*, XLVII, 10, 17, 3: *Crescit enim contumelia ex persona eius qui contumelian fecit.* If this was also the principle underlying Attic law, we have the explanation of the double penalty mentioned in Lysias X, 19 (cited above, p. 59n); i.e., a personal injury caused by a slave is a graver injury. Glotz, *loc. cit.*, regards such double penalties as the price of buying off vengeance. Unfortunately we have no evidence as to how Attic law punished offenses by slaves against the person of freemen (except for the fragments of Lysias above mentioned). The *Papyrus Halensis* shows that Alexandrian law of the third century punished a slave with a hundred stripes for striking or threatening to strike a freeman; a freeman for the same offense, pays a fine of a hundred drachmae. If the master compounds for the injury done by his slave, he pays two hundred drachmae, or double the fine imposed on the

Besides the severity of these punishments, one further feature deserves notice: viz. the recognition and embodiment of the principle of private vengeance. In most cases the person injured (or his surviving representative, if it is a case of murder) is entrusted with the administration of the penalty. The only exception is found in IX, 872bc; and here the public executioner is under the direction of the victim's avenger (ὁ ἑλών), who determines how many stripes are to be inflicted. Platonic law in this respect diverges strikingly from Attic law. Though in Attic law a trial for murder was a private action and had to be instituted by a representative of the murdered man, yet the sentence was executed by the state officials. Thus Antiphon tells us expressly and emphatically that not even slaves who had murdered their masters, even when they have been caught in the act, are allowed to be put to death by the dead man's relatives, but are delivered to the authorities "in accordance with your ancestral laws."[46] This shows clearly the law of the late fifth century, and Antiphon's language implies that even then this procedure was of considerable antiquity. Attic law, therefore, had long got beyond the principle of allowing the injured party or his representative to exact the penalty from the wrong-doer. Plato's law on this point represents most decidedly a step backward.

One further detail of the law of *αἰκία* deserves comment. Besides being whipped, the slave must be kept in irons until the injured person consents to his release. What is the significance of this addition? Such a provision is not found in any historical code,[47] and may be Plato's own invention. The slave's usefulness to his master during this period would be somewhat impaired, though not entirely so; slaves often worked in irons, especially when there was danger of a revolt, as in the Attic mines, or when the slave was a particularly vicious one. But the slave who had to be kept in irons was regarded as a lower sort of being than the ordinary slave. This consideration, and the fact that it is the slave who has to gain the pardon of the man he has injured, suggest that it was part of Plato's intention here to make the slave experience a kind of degradation analogous to the

---

freeman (Meyer, p. 241). Thus the principle enunciated by Ulpian would seem to have been recognized by Alexandrian law.

[46] Antiphon V, 48: *καίτοι οὐδὲ οἱ τοὺς δεσπότας ἀποκτείναντες, ἐὰν ἐπ' αὐτοφώρῳ ληφθῶσιν, οὐδ' οὗτοι ἀποθνήσκουσιν ὑπ' αὐτῶν τῶν προσηκόντων, ἀλλὰ παραδιδόασιν αὐτοὺς τῇ ἀρχῇ κατὰ νόμους ὑμετέρους πατρίους.*

[47] Partsch, *Archiv*, VI, 67, calls it "eine Massgabe, die wenig nach einem geschichtlichen Vorbild aussieht." Cf. *Dikaiomata*, p. 110.

ἀτιμία, or loss of civic rights, incurred by the free citizen for certain offenses.

There are cases, indeed, in which the punishment of slaves under Platonic law is markedly milder than the punishment of citizens for the same offenses. A slave who takes public property is to be flogged or fined (if this second alternative is not to be taken as applying only to the *metics*, to whom the law also applies), but a citizen is to be put to death (XII, 941d). And a slave guilty of temple-robbery is to be branded, flogged, and driven across the border, whereas a citizen is to be put to death (IX, 854d). The penalties in these cases are the same for the slave and for the freeman who is not a citizen. As before remarked, the fact of citizenship implies special responsibility, and for offenses against the public, such as these, the citizen is held more severely to account. What is mere robbery for the non-citizen is treason in the citizen.[48]

(4) In so far as Plato's law regards the slave as capable of knowing the distinction between lawful and unlawful conduct and holds him liable in his own person for breaches of the law, we can say that it recognizes his "personality." But the motive of protecting the master's property interest in his slave often prevents the full development of this principle. This is especially true with respect to the first two classes of offenses, where the slave's liability to punishment can always be extinguished, if the master pleases to compound for the injuries he has done. With respect to the last two classes of offenses the master has no right to come between the slave and the legal consequences of his actions; and here the slave's legal personality stands out most clearly. With respect to homicide and offenses against the public not only do we find the slave required to bear the full legal consequences of his acts, but also entitled to some share of legal capacity in defending himself. Certain phrases in Plato's text show us that the slave is entitled to trial, and in the ordinary courts, for these offenses. The slave is regarded as the defendant (ἐὰν δὲ δοῦλος . . . ἀποκτείνῃ καὶ ὄφλῃ τὴν δίκην, IX, 872b); and there are references to judges (τοῖς δικασταῖς, IX, 854d) and to judgment by a court (ἐν δικαστηρίῳ, ἡ κρίσις, XII, 941d).[49] The slave may bear

---

[48] Cf. also IX, 881d, where the law forbidding eating or drinking or otherwise associating with a person convicted of ἀσέβεια refers only to freemen. It seems to be assumed that such an exile will need the services of slaves, hence the law does not apply to them.

[49] Cf. also XII 954e: ἐάν τίς τινα δίκῃ παραγενέσθαι κωλύσῃ βίᾳ, εἴτε αὐτὸν εἴτε μάρτυρας, ἐὰν μὲν δοῦλον . . . ἐὰν δὲ ἐλεύθερον κτλ. If the antithesis δοῦλον . . . ἐλεύθερον be taken to refer

witness in a murder trial and may be sued, like any free man, for false testimony (XI, 937ab). These scattered references to a kind of legal personality possessed by the slave are the more significant in that they are casually introduced, for the most part, thus implying that the slave's standing before the law of Plato's πόλις is far from being that of a mere thing subject to ownership; and implying also that the writer is speaking of usages both familiar and obvious to his readers. Apart from other evidence, this would lead us to make certain inferences regarding Attic law. But we know from other sources that for capital offenses the slave was entitled to trial at Athens,[50] and Demosthenes shows us that a slave could even be defendant in a private suit affecting property.[51] Thus it is fully in the spirit of Attic legislation that the law of the *Lille Papyrus* permits in certain cases a suit to be brought against a slave "as if he were a freeman" (ὡς ἐλευθέρῳ).[52] Of course in such private suits the master was also indirectly the defendant, since he was liable for whatever damages the slave was unable to pay, at least to the value of the slave; and if it was shown that the slave was acting under his orders his liability would be complete.[53] Nevertheless even this limited legal capacity accorded the slave in Greek law is significant by comparison with the practice of Roman law, which regarded the slave as completely devoid of legal personality.[54]

---

to principals as well as witnesses, this passage also implies that a slave can be a defendant at law.

[50] Antiphon V, 47, 48; Isocrates *Panath.* 181.

[51] Dem. XXXVII, 22, 51; LV, 31, 34; Lipsius, 795; Beauchet II, 458–459; Partsch, *Bürgschaftsrecht*, p. 135, note 10. Harpocration (Bekker 141, 6) speaks of αἱ πρὸς τοὺς δούλους δίκαι.

[52] Col. I, lines 1–3 (Meyer, p. 245).

[53] Cf. the words διώκειν ἐμέ in Dem. XXXVII, 51, which deals with a suit brought against a slave; likewise καταδεδιῄτηταί μου in Dem. LV, 31.

[54] Sohm-Mitteis-Wenger, *Institutionen*, pp. 167–168.

Chapter V

THE LEGAL CAPACITY OF SLAVES

We have seen in the preceding chapter that the slave is capable of being a defendant at law.[1] With this *passive Prozessfähigkeit*, as Wenger calls it, we are not here concerned. The question now to be examined is the extent and nature of the slave's active legal capacity, that is, the extent of his power to bring suit or take other legal steps for the protection of his own rights or the rights of others.

There are several passages in Plato's law implying that the slave can in some sense own property. We hear of fines imposed on slaves (τί χρὴ παθεῖν ἢ τίνα ζημίαν ἀποτίνειν, XII, 941d). In another case the slave who denounces the seller of adulterated or spurious goods is allowed to take the goods in question as his reward (XI, 917d). This implies that the slave's possessions are in some sense distinct from his master's. There would be little efficacy in the reward offered for denunciation if the confiscated goods were merely appropriated by the slave for his master. Nor would the payment of a fine be a penalty if what the law takes from the slave is not his own but his master's. Again we hear of "slave and *metic* hirelings" (μισθωτοὶ δοῦλοι καὶ ἔποικοι, V, 742a), a phrase which, taken in connection with the foregoing passages, certainly suggests the payment of wages to a slave workman as to a free *metic*.

These fragments of legislation have their historical parallels in Greek (above all in Attic) law. The Athenian building inscriptions seem to indicate that slave and free workmen labored side by side, receiving the same pay and doing the same work.[2] The Old Oligarch comments on the wealthy slaves living at Athens and says it is a cardinal principle of Athenian policy to allow their slaves to acquire possessions (χρήματα) and live in luxury and even magnificence.[3] Aeschines describes with indignation the conduct of a public slave named Pittalacus who had "plenty of money" (εὐπορῶν ἀργυρίου).[4] Many of the slaves at Athens lived apart from their masters (the δοῦλοι μισθοφοροῦντες to whom we have previously referred), conducting businesses of their own and paying their masters a certain proportion of their earnings.[5] And the purchase of his freedom by a slave was a common occurrence at Athens.[6] In Menander's recently

[1] See above, p. 71. [2] Zimmern, *Greek Commonwealth*, pp. 257–258; *CIA*, I, 324.
[3] [Xen.] *Const. of Athens* I, 11. [4] *Timarchus* 54.
[5] On these χωρὶς οἰκοῦντες see above, p. 18, n. 5. [6] See below, p. 98.

recovered comedy Ἐπιτρέποντες two slaves dispute about the ownership of certain trinkets and refer the matter to an arbitrator, just as two freemen might have done. Turning to other Greek cities, we find that the law of Gortyn imposes fines upon slaves,[7] and declares that the cattle and sheep of a serf (οἰκεύς) are not to be reckoned as part of the master's estate.[8] An inscription from Pergamum (second century) prescribes that a slave who pollutes a public well shall be punished by the confiscation of his possessions (ὧν ἂν ἔχῃ στερέσθω), besides being flogged.[9] In the papyri, especially where Graeco-Egyptian, as distinct from Roman law is in question, there are likewise numerous references to the property of slaves.[10]

On the face of this evidence we would seem to be justified in asserting that Greek law recognized the property of slaves. But this interpretation has been disputed. Beauchet holds that since the slave had no legal personality, his χρήματα were nothing more than the *peculium* of the Roman slave, i.e. possessions which could be confiscated by his master. At the same time he admits that custom and the enlightened self-interest of slave-owners (especially at Athens) allowed the Greek slave considerably more independence in the use of his possessions than was allowed the Roman slave.[11] This view almost begs the question, since the point at issue is precisely what degree of legal personality was possessed by the Greek slave. At the same time one must grant that a right of ownership is scarcely to be called such unless there goes with it a right to take some kind of legal action to protect one's ownership. If the Greek slave was forced to rely upon his master for the protection of his interests there is little meaning in saying that he was capable of ownership in his own right.

There is one passage in the *Laws* (but not a conclusive one)

---

[7] Col. II, lines 8 ff., 27 ff. (Bücheler-Zitelmann, pp. 19 f.).

[8] Col. IV, lines 31 ff. A later decree (No. 8 in Kohler-Ziebarth) contains provisions protecting the slave against robbery by his master.

[9] *OG.* No. 483, lines 172–183.

[10] Taubenschlag, in *ZSS*, Rom. Abt., L (1930) 156 ff. See also p. 157, n. 5, for evidence that slaves could own property under Babylonian, Assyrian, and Jewish law.

[11] II, 444–448. Wallon (*Histoire de l'esclavage dans l'antiquité* I, 291) asserts that the slave is incapable of ownership, but later modifies this view. The property of slaves was an exception, but "*assez générale.*" This is a good illustration of the difficulty of understanding Greek law when we start from Roman premises. Wallon begins by assuming that the slave is merely property and draws the logical consequences; hence whatever does not conform to these consequences is regarded as an "exception." Another vitiating feature of his procedure is his use of Roman comedy as a source of information about the Greek slave. The result is still further to confound Roman and Greek law.

indicating that the slave could take action on his own initiative to secure redress for injuries done him. In the account of the duties of the rural magistrates we are told that they have power to judge minor disputes, whether the parties be slaves or freemen.[12] Unfortunately for clarity the alternative "whether slave or freeman" is so stated as to apply strictly only to the persons accused, not to the accusers. If the passage be taken, as I think most readers would take it, as applying both to accusers and accused, then it recognizes the right of the slave to go before the *Agronomoi* and appeal for justice. And if the rural slave could thus appeal to the *Agronomoi*, doubtless also the city slave could appeal to the *Agoranomoi* and the *Astynomoi*, since the magisterial functions of these three boards of officers are in other respects so similar (XI, 913d). The right to make accusations before a magistrate is, as we shall soon see, accorded the slave for other purposes in the *Laws*, so that he is not altogether ἀπρόσωπος, and I see no reason why we should not take Plato's law at its face value as granting him this rudimentary sort of legal capacity for the protection of his own interests. Though the action the slave can take is limited (there is no hint that he can bring suit in the courts like a freeman), it is enough to establish the principle of his capacity for ownership in his own right.

Under Attic law we might suppose the slave to be incapable of even this limited range of legal action if we take literally a passage in another of Plato's dialogues which says that the slave, when he is injured or reviled, is unable to help himself or anyone else for whom he cares.[13] But it is hard to reconcile this with the evidence of the power to sue and be sued exercized by the slaves at Athens who conducted businesses on their own account.[14] If Plato's statement is not a rhetorical exaggeration, it must be taken as applying only to the slaves who were under the direct supervision of their masters, not to the δοῦλοι μισθοφοροῦντες.[15] And it is certainly hard to believe that the rich slaves at Athens would have been as fearless as the Old Oligarch tells us they were if they had not enjoyed a large measure of power to protect themselves and their property by legal methods.[16] The law of Gortyn permitted the slave to claim protection from his master and even proceed at law against him. The female

---

[12] VI, 761de: γειτόνων δὲ καὶ τῶν ἄλλων πολιτῶν ἣν ἄλλος ἄλλον ἀδικῇ, δοῦλος ἢ ἐλεύθερος, δικάζοντας κτλ. [13] *Gorg.* 483b (cited above, p. 55n).

[14] Beauchet, II, 461; Lipsius, p. 797.

[15] Partsch, *Griechisches Bürgschaftsrecht*, pp. 137–138. [16] [Xen.] *Const. of Athens* I, 11.

slave is even entitled to damages from her master if he has assaulted her.[17] In the Graeco-Egyptian law of the papyri a slave could appear before a magistrate to make a claim, either for himself or for his master, in cases of personal injury or property damage,[18] a procedure parallel to that suggested by the above mentioned passage from the *Laws*. What evidence there is, then, points to the fact that Greek law regarded the slave as capable of ownership and put some legal remedies (though in most cases inadequate ones, no doubt) at his disposal for protecting his right of ownership. In this respect there seems to be a clear difference between Greek and Roman law.

We hear more about the slave's power of legal action when the public welfare is concerned. The slave has the right of *μήνυσις*, i.e. he may lodge information with the magistrates regarding an offense against the public which he knows to have been committed. Thus he may denounce the sale of adulterated or spurious goods (XI, 917d), the neglect of parents (XI, 932d), and the appropriation of buried treasure (XI, 914a). The slave who denounces is rewarded; in the first of the above cases he receives the goods in question; in the other two cases he is set free. The slave who fails to denounce the appropriation of buried treasure is punished with death. Probably it is only an oversight that the death penalty is not also prescribed for failing to denounce the neglect of parents. No penalty is specified for false denunciation.

The *μήνυσις* of slaves was recognized in Attic law.[19] The informer merely gave the magistrates information of the breach of the law. If the officers thought fit to press the case, accusers were appointed and the prosecution was instituted by them, not by the informer. It was on the basis of denunciation made by slaves and aliens that Alcibiades and his associates were prosecuted for the mutilation of the Hermae.[20] And Attic law rewarded a slave informer with freedom, at least when the crime denounced was a grave one.[21] In the fifth century death seems to have been the penalty for false denunciation, but this law seems to have been repealed.[22] We hear of *μήνυσις* in Attic law only in connection with the crimes of treason, sacrilege, and theft of public money. Besides the offenses mentioned above, Plato

[17] Col. II, lines 7 ff. (Bücheler-Zitelmann, p. 19).

[18] Taubenschlag, in *ZSS*, Rom. Abt. L (1930), 163.

[19] Lipsius, pp. 208 f.; Bonner, *Evidence in Athenian Courts*, pp. 39 f. We hear also of rewards for denunciation at Ceos (Ziebarth, in *Hermes*, XXXII (1897), 612 f.) and in the papyri (Taubenschlag, in *ZSS*, Rom. Abt., L (1930), 165).

[20] Thuc. VI, 27, 28; Plutarch *Alcibiades* 19.

[21] Lysias V, 5; VII, 16; Antiphon V, 34.

[22] Andocides I, 20.

mentions denunciation in connection with the following crimes: possessing more property than the maximum allowed (V, 745a); possessing foreign currency (V, 742b); and sacrilege (X, 907e, 910c). Doubtless it is only an accident that no mention is made of slaves or slave-denunciation in these cases. It would seem, therefore, that Plato used the device of denunciation, both by slaves and by freemen, much more extensively than was done in Attic law. It would also seem that the addition of a penalty for failure to denounce is Plato's own invention. Attic law seems to have relied entirely upon rewards.

Under certain circumstances the slave can give testimony in court: "A slave man or slave woman or a child shall be allowed to testify (*μαρτυρεῖν*) and speak in court (*συνηγορεῖν*) only at trials for murder, and only if they produce sufficient sureties that they will remain for trial in case they should be charged with giving false testimony" (XI, 937ab). Just what does Plato mean by *μαρτυρεῖν*? It is evident at once that he is not using the word in the sense of *μηνύειν*; for we have seen that a slave is allowed to give *μήνυσις* of various offenses against the laws, whereas the passage under examination says that slaves are to give evidence (*μαρτυρεῖν*) only in cases of murder. Besides this, the slave is liable to a suit for perjury (*δίκη ψευδομαρτυριῶν*), which shows that his standing was that of a witness.[23] What precisely is the difference between an informer and a witness? In the first place (here Platonic law and Attic law are in accord), the informer appears before a magistrate or a board of magistrates,[24] the witness appears before a court. For trivial offenses over which the magistrates have jurisdiction this distinction would be of little importance; but for the graver offenses (and these in the main are those for which *μήνυσις* was prescribed) the distinction between an informer and a witness would be quite marked. In Athens the assertions of an informer did not automatically come before a court of law. They were first submitted to an examination by the officials, and only if they were found sufficiently credible (probably only if other substantiating evidence was discovered) was an indictment brought against the person denounced.[25] The assertions

[23] See Rentsch, *De δίκη ψευδομαρτυριῶν*, pp. 14–15.

[24] For Platonic law the expressions *ἐναντίον τῶν ἀρχόντων* (XI, 917 d), *ἀγγελλέτω τοῖς ἀστυνόμοις . . . τοῖς ἀγρονόμοις* (XI, 913d, 914a), and *ἐξαγγελλέτω τοῖς ἄρχουσι* (XI, 932d) are decisive. For Attic law see Kroll, in Pauly-Wissowa, *s.v. μήνυσις*.

[25] Guggenheim, *Die Bedeutung der Folterung im Attischen Prozess*, p. 8; Lipsius, pp. 209 f. Thucydides VI, 53, says that the information about the mutilation of the Hermae was not subjected to the *δοκιμασία*, implying that the procedure was unusual.

of a witness were not required to undergo this preliminary scrutiny. Provided they were made by a person competent to be a witness, and provided also they were relevant to the matter at issue, they were submitted without further question to the judgment of the court.[26] This standing of the slave witness before the court is emphasized in Plato's text by the additional provision that he can plead (*συνηγορεῖν*) as well as testify for his principal. In Attic law the *συνήγορος* was one who spoke before the court in support of one of the litigants. The *συνηγορία* might be a legal plea based on the evidence already submitted, it might be an appeal for a favorable decision because of the speaker's past services to the state, or it might contain statements of facts relevant to the issue, sometimes even a repetition of evidence already given.[27] In other words, it might be little more than an extended or informal form of *μαρτυρία*. Doubtless this was what the slave's *συνηγορεῖν* in Plato's law was intended to be.

But the slave witness was not on an equality with the free witness, for the slave was required to provide surety that he would remain to stand trial if there should be a suit for perjury. The *δίκη ψευδομαρτυριῶν* was a remedy provided by Attic law,[28] as well as by Platonic law. It appears that after the evidence was in and before the judges proceeded to vote, the opportunity was given the litigants to challenge any point of the evidence submitted; and this challenge would furnish the basis of a *δίκη ψευδομαρτυριῶν*, which however, would come to trial only after the conclusion of the original suit.[29] Hence the reason for the provision in Plato's text requiring the slave witness to furnish surety. We may safely assume, with Rentsch,[30] that a similar provision was found in Attic law with respect to slaves. The liability of the slave to the *δίκη ψευδομαρτυριῶν* is one of several instances in which the slave can be a defendant under Platonic law.[31] As to the penalties for giving false testimony, Plato's law provides that a person twice convicted of *ψευδομαρτυριῶν* can no longer be compelled to testify, and one thrice convicted is not to be allowed

[26] Bonner, pp. 14 ff., 27 ff. Whether the informer appeared in court or not would depend upon the nature of his information and on his competence to be a witness. And he would appear, strictly speaking, not as an informer but as a witness.

[27] Lipsius, pp. 906 ff.; Bonner and Smith, II, 8 ff.

[28] On this suit see Rentsch, *op. cit.*; Lipsius, pp. 778 ff.; Bonner and Smith, II, 261 ff.; Bonner, pp. 88 ff.; and above, p. 61. This suit was allowable, not only for false testimony given in court, but also for other false depositions of affidavits. But there is no indication that it was allowed for false *μήνυσις*. As Aristotle puts it (*Rhet.* 1376a 12) the witness bears some of the risks of the trial. The informer apparently did not.

[29] Arist. *Const. of Athens* p. 104 (ed. Blass-Thalheim).

[30] *Op. cit.*, 15. [31] See above, p. 71.

to testify (XI, 937c). This provision would presumably apply to slaves as well as free witnesses. Attic law imposed full *ἀτιμία* in such cases,[32] which would seem to be a much heavier penalty, though the whole question of the import of *ἀτιμία* in Attic law is obscure. Besides this, Attic law also imposed a fine upon a convicted perjurer.[33] This does not appear in Plato's law, though it is hard to think that it is an intentional omission. Nor does Plato say anything regarding the responsibility of the master in case his slave is convicted of *ψευδομαρτυριῶν*, though the master must have been in some sense responsible for this as for the other unlawful acts committed by his slaves.

To what extent is the slave a compellable, as well as a competent witness in Platonic law? The freeman is required to appear as a witness, or else take an oath in disclaimer (XI, 936e). In the case of the slave the matter is more complicated, by virtue of the fact that he is subject to his master as well as to the state. It is clear, however, that in at least some situations Plato intends that the master shall have no right to prevent his slave's appearance in court. A law provides that if anyone by force prevents a slave from coming to court, whether principal or witness, whether his own or another's, the suit shall be dismissed (XII, 954e).[34] Unfortunately this law can hardly be taken as applying to all possible cases in which a slave witness might be detained from court, for to take it so would lead to some impossible results.[35] Evidently some tacit limitation is implied

[32] Rentsch, p. 44; Bonner and Smith, II, 262 ff.

[33] Antiphon II, iv, 7: *οἱ μὲν γὰρ [ἐλεύθεροι] ἀτιμοῦνταί τε καὶ χρήμασι ζημιοῦνται, ἐὰν μὴ τἀληθῆ δοκῶσι μαρτυρῆσαι.* Rentsch, p. 52; Bonner and Smith, II, 262 ff.

[34] XII, 954e: *ἐάν τίς τινα δίκῃ παραγενέσθαι κωλύσῃ βίᾳ, εἴτε αὐτὸν εἴτε μάρτυρας, ἐὰν μὲν δοῦλον εἴτε αὐτοῦ εἴτε ἀλλότριον, ἀτελῆ καὶ ἄκυρον γίγνεσθαι τὴν δίκην.*

[35] There are eight possible cases, as follows:

A. The slave a witness for the prosecution.
  AA. The master preventing.
    AAA. The master not the defendant.
    AAB. The master the defendant.
  AB. Some person other than the master preventing.
    ABA. This person the defendant.
    ABB. This person not a party to the trial.
B. The slave a witness for the defense.
  BA. The master preventing.
    BAA. The master not the prosecutor.
    BAB. The master the prosecutor.
  BB. Some person other than the master preventing.
    BBA. This person the prosecutor.
    BBB. This person not a party to the trial.

Assuming that in each case the dismissal of the suit is the only legal consequence of preventing

here, and we must endeavor to see what it is. The dismissal of the suit is clearly intended as a penalty, and obviously the prosecutor would suffer. We may then take it as certain that the prosecutor would have no right to prevent any slave witnesses, no matter to whom they belonged, from appearing in court.[36] Even if the prosecutor's own slave has been summoned by the defendant, he has no right to detain him. For the defendant, however, the dismissal of the suit would obviously be an advantage, and it would be absurd to interpret this law as permitting a defendant to reap an advantage from an act of violence (*βίᾳ*). The law then can be clearly taken to mean only that the defendant has the right to summon the prosecutor's slave. Would the prosecutor likewise have the right to summon the defendant's slave? And could either party summon a slave belonging to some one not concerned in the litigation? These are questions which Plato's text does not answer. It might be inferred that if a master had no right to prevent the appearance of his slave as a witness against himself, *a fortiori* he could not refuse to allow his slave to testify in cases in which he was not involved. But in view of the master's probable liability if the slave is sued for false testimony, even this inference is a hazardous one.

A further question now arises. In what form would slave evidence be laid before the court? Attic law permitted slave testimony (with the possible exception of testimony in a murder case) only when given under torture.[37] This curious belief that the assertions of slaves can be credited only when given under physical pain (the one case, Mahaffy says,[38] in which real stupidity can be attributed to the Greeks) has its parallel in the procedure of Roman law. Plato, however, says nothing about the torture (*βάσανος*) of slaves. He may, of course, be taking this institution for granted. But there are several considerations that dispose of this assumption. If the slave is accorded the freeman's privilege of making a *συνηγορία* in court, it would be strange if he were not also allowed to testify like a freeman. In Attic procedure the evidence of slaves given under torture appeared in court only indirectly, through the testimony of

a slave witness from appearing in court it follows: (a) If the master of the slave is not a party to the suit, it is necessary to get his consent before the slave can be used as a witness (cases AAA, BAA); (b) Any person, not a party to the trial can prevent the use of any slave, his own or another's, as witness (cases ABB, BBB); (c) The defendant may summon the prosecutor's slave, but the prosecutor may not summon the defendant's slave (cases BAB, AAB); (d) The prosecutor may not use any slave witness, not even his own, unless the other party consents (cases AAA, AAB, ABA, ABB).

[36] Cases BAB and BBA.

[37] Bonner, p. 34; Guggenheim, pp. 2 ff.

[38] *Social Life in Greece*, p. 241.

those who had witnessed the torture. The free witness, even though he had already given his testimony before the magistrates at the preliminary hearing (the ἀνάκρισις) or at the preliminary trial before the arbitrators, was required to give it again in court at the final trial.[39] Βάσανοι, or answers of slaves to questions put them under torture, were presented to the court only through the testimony of those who had witnessed the torture. It would be a strange departure from Attic procedure for Plato to prescribe the *βάσανος* for slaves and at the same time give them standing before the court. But the conclusive argument is the fact that the slave witness is liable to a *δίκη ψευδομαρτυριῶν*. The testimony given under torture does not seem to have been open to legal challenge;[40] and it was one of the oratorical commonplaces of the fourth century that the *βάσανος* was an infallible method of eliciting the truth. Slave evidence given under torture even had the curious legal effect of protecting a witness who gave similar evidence from prosecution for perjury.[41] This constitutes decisive evidence that Plato intends that the slave witness shall give his testimony like a freeman, not under torture.

Since the slave witness is not put to the torture, would he be required to take an oath under Plato's law? In Attic law all witnesses and principals in murder trials were required at the preliminary investigation to take a solemn oath.[42] In other cases the oath of witnesses was apparently not required, though it was sometimes given.[43] Nothing is said in the *Laws* about the oaths of witnesses, beyond the provision that an oath in disclaimer must be taken by any person summoned to give testimony who denies having any knowledge of the facts in the case. Plato forbids the use of the party oath, i.e. the oath taken by the litigants themselves as to the truth of their contentions.[44] This is an archaic form of procedure which Plato says is inadequate now that some men no longer believe in the gods, and others think that the gods pay no attention to human affairs or that their wrath can be easily appeased (XII, 948b ff.). But the oath is prescribed (1) for judges (*δικασταί*), (2) for those voting for

[39] Evidence was generally given orally down to 378–377 B.C., as Bonner has shown (pp. 54 ff.). After that date evidence in the heliastic courts was presented in the form of a written deposition read by the clerk, the witness being present and formally certifying that it was his testimony. But in the homicide courts evidence continued to be presented orally. Bonner and Smith, I, pp. 353 ff.

[40] Isaeus VIII, 12; Dem. XXX, 37; Isocrates XXI, 4; XVII, 54.

[41] Bonner, p. 74; and Isocrates XVII, 54.

[42] Antiphon V, 12, 15; Lysias IV, 4; Antiphon I, 28.

[43] Bonner, pp. 76 ff.; Bonner and Smith, II, 173.

[44] Bonner and Smith, II, 161 ff.

public officers, (3) for "judges" (*κριταί*) in musical and athletic contests, and for all other cases in which there is no profit in false swearing (XII, 949a). This general principle would seem to imply that witnesses, in some cases at least, might be required to take oath; and we have seen that the oath in disclaimer is explicitly prescribed. Clearly we cannot say, with Bonner,[45] that Plato abolishes the witness oath, though there is no evidence that he requires it, even in murder cases. The law of Gortyn shows that the taking of an oath by a slave was not unknown in Greek law, and Plato had a great admiration for Cretan legislation.[46]

It should be noted that the privilege accorded a slave of testifying without torture in a trial for murder is not altogether an anomaly in Platonic law (nor in Attic law, either, if it was permitted in Attic law). For the slave had the right to give information to the magistrates of offenses (some of them capital) committed by freemen, and the slave informer was not put to the torture.[47] It was the policy of Platonic law (and also of Attic law) to encourage slaves to give information, by promising them freedom or gifts of money, and to require that this information be given under torture would be to nullify such a policy. Unless we assume that in the actual prosecution of an offender the information supplied by the slave was not admissible in court (an unlikely assumption), then we must admit that sometimes in other than murder cases slave evidence not given under torture was allowable. Of course the slave in such cases was not a witness, in the strict sense of the word, for he did not appear in court, and was not liable to prosecution for giving false evidence; but the principle involved is not essentially different.[48]

---

[45] *Op. cit.* p. 71.

[46] Not only did the law of Gortyn permit a slave-woman to take oath to an assault upon her by her master, but it also provided that in such cases the oath of the slave-woman was to prevail over that of the master. Col. II, lines 12 ff.: *ὁρκιοτέραν δ'ἔμεν τὰν δόλαν.*

[47] Bonner, p. 39; Guggenhem, p. 6.

[48] It is clear that Plato uses the word *μαρτυρεῖν* in these passages in its precise legal sense. The fourth-century writers frequently make a distinction between *βάσανοι* and *μαρτυρίαι*, and between *βασανισθέντες* and *μαρτυρήσαντες*. See the passages cited above, p. 81, and also Aristotle's enumeration of the five kinds of *πίστεις* in *Rhet.* 1375a 23: *νόμοι, μάρτυρες, συνθῆκαι βάσανοι, ὅρκοι.* (Cf. also the *Rhet. ad Alex.* 1442b 37, 1428a 23, 1443b 28). It would seem that in the strict sense of the word neither the slave-informer nor the slave put to the torture could be called a *μάρτυς*. But the word *μαρτυρεῖν* and its cognate terms are often used more loosely. Demosthenes speaks of the torture (*βάσανος*) as the most accurate kind of evidence (*ἀκριβεστάτη μαρτυρία*, LIX, 122: cf. also XLVII, 8; XXXIV, 31; LIII, 22); and even Aristotle, after having carefully distinguished *βάσανοι* and *μαρτυρίαι* as distinct kinds of *πίστεις*, or means of legal persuasion, goes on to use language which implies that *βάσανοι* are a species of *μαρτυρίαι* (*Rhet.* 1376b 33). This use of *μαρτυρίαι*, now in a generic, now in a specific sense, has led to confusion. It is important to note that Plato's usage is above reproach from the legal point of view.

What now about Attic law? Plato's recognition of the slave's competence as a witness in murder cases is so interesting that we should like to know whether it is his own invention, or whether he is copying the procedure of his native city. Clearly we cannot take Plato's text as evidence for Attic law, as has sometimes been done. For as Guggenheim has pointed out,[49] the passage in which this provision occurs contains other provisions that are known to be departures from Attic law, viz. the right of a woman over forty years of age to testify in court and, if she be unmarried, to bring suit. We may add also that even if Attic law did permit a slave to give evidence, the *καὶ συνηγορεῖν* of Plato's text is something additional. If Plato modified Attic law in these respects, it is possible that he did so likewise in permitting a slave to be a witness.

Apart from Plato, we have the testimony of the fifth-century orator Antiphon, who clearly says that a slave is allowed to give evidence against a freeman in a case of murder.[50] Three other orations of Antiphon speak of slave testimony (*μαρτυρία*) and slave witnesses (*μάρτυρες*).[51] But the meaning of these assertions has been a matter of considerable controversy. Lipsius interpreted them to mean that in a trial for murder the usual requirement of the torture was waived and a slave was allowed to testify like a freeman,[52] which is essentially the principle adopted by Plato. But this view has been vigorously challenged by Guggenheim and Bonner, who contend that in these passages Antiphon is using *μαρτυρεῖν* in the sense of *μηνύειν*. They also point out the absence of slave witnesses in the murder trials to which Antiphon's orations refer, and in some of them the lack of slave witnesses is difficult to explain, if Attic law recognized any such principle as that embodied in Plato's law. Since Antiphon is our only authority to suggest that Attic law permitted this unusual procedure in murder cases, they conclude that it was an invariable rule of Attic law that the testimony of slaves, to be admissible in court, must be given under torture.[53]

Let us consider first the contention that Antiphon is using *μαρτυρεῖν* in the sense of *μηνύειν*. This view was most fully expounded by Guggenheim, though it was adopted (I think without due criticism) by Bonner. Since none of our other texts say anything

---

[49] *Op. cit.*, p. 13.

[50] Antiphon V, 48: *εἴπερ γὰρ καὶ μαρτυρεῖν ἔξεστι δούλῳ κατὰ τοῦ ἐλευθέρου τὸν φόνον κτλ.*

[51] I, 30; II, iii, 4; VI, 23.

[52] Lipsius, p. 873; also Leisi, *Der Zeuge im Attischen Recht*, pp. 12 ff., 21 ff.

[53] Bonner, pp. 34 ff.; Guggenheim, pp. 7 ff.; Wyse, in *Class. Rev.* XX (1906), 59; Thiel, *Antiphons Erste Tetralogie*, pp. 81 ff. Bonner and Smith, II, 223 ff.

about μήνυσις in murder cases, Guggenheim endeavors to prove that Attic law permitted μήνυσις of murder. He points out that the slave "evidence" mentioned in Antiphon I, 30, and that on which the arguments of the First Tetralogy are based, are not evidence, in the strict sense of testimony before a court, but information given prior to the beginning of legal action. In both cases, therefore, Antiphon is using μαρτυρία in the sense of information which can be used as the basis of an action, rather than testimony brought out in court to support a legal contention. This is true enough, but is far from proving that such information can technically be identified with the μήνυσις of Attic law. Μήνυσις was laid before a magistrate, and concerned an offense against the public which could be proceeded against by a γραφή or some other form of prosecution open to any qualified citizen.[54] But there was no γραφὴ φόνου in Attic law; homicide remained a private wrong which could be proceeded against only by some relative of the victim. Information of murder would therefore be laid, not before a magistrate (for he had no power to prosecute) but only before some relative of the victim, who alone could make use of it. If then what Antiphon calls μαρτυρία is properly only to be called information, it is information of an extra-judicial sort, not the μήνυσις of Attic law. But if this view is adopted, then it is pointless for Antiphon to assert that a slave can give evidence against a free man in a case of murder. For information of this sort is extra-judicial, involves no legal consequences, and therefore requires no legal authorization.

Since Antiphon's statement is certainly not so pointless as it would be on this interpretation, let us ask what more it can mean. Let us assume, for example, that a slave whose master has been murdered goes to a relative of the victim and tells what he knows. And let us assume also that the slave is the only person (apart from the murderer) who knows the facts of the case. If the relative is to institute action against the murderer he must do so on the basis of the information supplied by the slave. Either, then, Attic law did not allow an action in such a case, or the prosecutor could make legal use of the slave's information. The only way in which he could make legal use of it was to bring it before the court as evidence in the judicial sense. And this is what I think Antiphon must mean. It is true that the statements of the slave at first are not evidence, in the judicial sense, but merely information of an extra-judicial sort; but

[54] See above, p. 76.

when such information is put to legal use it becomes testimony, in the judicial sense. In other words, the slave can be a witness in the strict sense of the word.

Must we assume that in the hypothetical case mentioned above this information supplied by the slave could take on the character of legal evidence only if reiterated under torture? Obviously if torture was required in such cases, few slaves would volunteer information, and a legal system designed to assist the apprehension and punishment of homicides would naturally be inclined to waive the requirement of the torture in such cases. We know also that the slave informer (in the technical sense of the word) was not put to the torture; and it would only be an extension of this principle to exempt from torture the slave who gave information of murder. This seems in fact to be asserted by Antiphon in the First Tetralogy: "In giving testimony of this sort [i.e. of murder], slaves are not put to the torture, but instead we give them their freedom."[55] The most natural interpretation of Antiphon leads us, then, to the conclusion that Attic law permitted information of murder supplied by slaves to be admitted in court, and that without torture.

Guggenheim, therefore, is correct in recognizing that there is a similarity between the cases of slave *μαρτυρία* mentioned by Antiphon and the slave *μήνυσις* of Attic law. This similarity consists in the fact that in both the slave gave information on which a legal action could be instituted, and in both cases this information was given without torture. But ignoring the fact that homicide was a private wrong in Attic law, Guggenheim failed to observe the legal differences between *μήνυσις* and information of murder. In the former case the information, being submitted to a public official, was subjected ordinarily to a *δοκιμασία*, or official examination, before action was instituted.[56] And if such information was relied upon in the later stages of the action, it was doubtless presented with some kind of official certification. But information of murder would be given only to a private individual; it would not therefore be subjected to official examination, and if it was to be put to any legal use at all it would have to take on all the status of evidence in the usual sense of the word. Thus slave-testimony, in the judicial sense of the word, is implied in the latter case, but not in the former.

---

[55] Antiphon II, iii, 4.

[56] Guggenheim admits (pp. 8–9) that this *δοκιμασία* is missing in the cases referred to by Antiphon.

Thus this exceptional procedure in cases of murder is due to the fact that prosecutions for homicide lay outside the competence of any but the relatives of the victim. If homicide had been regarded as an offense against the public and actionable by means of a *γραφή*, slaves who gave information of murder could have been treated exactly as slaves who informed of temple-robbing, or any other crime. But since homicide could be proceeded against only by private suit, it was necessary, if use was to be made of slave-information in apprehending and punishing offenders, to give the slave informer what looks like an anomalous status. But this apparent anomaly disappears, as we have seen, upon closer inspection. We can even say that to permit slaves to testify in murder cases was a step toward the assimilation of homicide to the class of offenses against the public as a wrong of sufficient public importance to justify exceptional procedure in punishing it.

But if it was a principle of Attic law that slaves could testify in murder cases, why do not slave witnesses actually appear in the trials in which Antiphon's orations figure? In two of these cases the lack of slave witnesses is at first sight surprising. In Antiphon's first oration the speaker is prosecuting his stepmother (through her *κύριος*, her son) for the murder of his father, and claims that the slaves in the household of the defendant could give evidence of the woman's previous attempt to poison his father. He says that he has challenged the defendant to put these slaves to the torture, but the challenge has not been accepted.[57] Why did the speaker resort to the *πρόκλησις εἰς βάσανον* if it was possible to obtain the slaves' testimony in court by the ordinary process of summoning them as witnesses? Is it that slaves are competent but not compellable witnesses? I think the explanation is to be found elsewhere. Gernet calls attention to the fact that no witnesses at all appear for the prosecution, and suggests that the reason is the requirement that witnesses in a murder trial had to take the same *διωμοσία* as the principal parties; in other words, the speaker's witnesses would have had to take a solemn oath as to the guilt of the accused, and they doubtless preferred to take the oath of disclaimer instead. This shows that the speaker's case was a weak one. In spite of his brave words about what the defendant's slaves knew, doubtless he dared not risk bringing them to the witness stand, not being sure what they would say when questioned. So he resorted to a familiar bluff, the chal-

[57] Antiphon I, 9–10.

lenge to the torture, and drew what profit he could from his opponent's refusal to accept the challenge.

In the sixth oration we have a different situation. The speaker himself is the defendant in a murder trial, and he claims that if his own slaves were put to the question they could give evidence establishing his innocence. He has offered them for examination, with or without torture, but the offer has been declined.[58] Why was it necessary for the speaker to acquiesce in the refusal of the prosecution to question these persons? We should especially note that the speaker mentions freemen as well as slaves whose testimony would be favorable to himself if only they were allowed to testify. Whatever be the explanation of this situation, it must lie in some disability which in this particular case affected free and slave witnesses alike. Consequently this case establishes no presumption as to the incompetence of slaves as witnesses. On the contrary, it appears from the text that if the prosecution had been willing, the defendant's slaves could have been questioned without the torture.[59]

Lastly, in the *Murder of Herodes*, the slave on whose assertions the murder charge against Euxitheus, the speaker, is based, has been put to death by his owners, the accusers of Euxitheus. It appears that the slave, when put to the torture privately by the prosecutors, at first accused Euxitheus of the murder but later retracted and asserted that Euxitheus was innocent. Euxitheus accuses his opponents of having put the slave to death to prevent his appearing in court.[60] This plainly suggests that the slave could have appeared as a witness. To be sure, Euxitheus speaks as if what he would have done, had the slave been still alive, is to demand that he be put to the torture, and not simply to summon him as a witness. But this case is unusual. The slave had already made contradictory statements, and consequently even Euxitheus, who expected the evidence to be favorable, might well prefer to have him put to the torture, in accordance with the prevailing opinion that the assertions of slaves were more worthy of credence when given under torture.[61]

Besides the orations of Antiphon, there are three orations of Lysias (I, XII, XIII) dealing with accusations of homicide; but in only the first of these, *On the Murder of Eratosthenes*, would there

[58] Antiphon VI, 22–23.

[59] Note especially *τοὺς δὲ δούλους, εἰ μὲν αὐτῷ ἐρωτῷντι τἀληθῆ δοκοῖεν λέγειν, εἰ δὲ μή, ἕτοιμος ἦ ἐκδιδόναι βασανίζειν*. The reference throughout is to procedure in court, as is shown by *ἐν τῷ δικαστηρίῳ*. [60] Antiphon V, 46: *καὶ διετείναντο αὐτὸν μὴ εἰσελθεῖν εἰς ὑμᾶς*.

[61] Dem. XLVII, 8; Lycurgus *Leocrates* 29; and the sources cited above in notes 40 and 48.

have been any possible occasion for slave testimony. In this case the relatives of Eratosthenes brought a charge of murder against Euphiletus, the speaker, in whose house the victim was done to death. Euphiletus claimed in his defense that Eratosthenes was guilty of adultery with his wife; that acting on a hint from his wife's maid, a slave girl, and accompanied by several of his friends as witnesses, he had broken in upon the lovers one evening, caught Eratosthenes *in flagrante delicto* and killed him. The prosecution however denied that there was adultery and asserted that Eratosthenes was enticed to the house and slain without cause. No use seems to be made of the slave girl's testimony in supporting these respective claims, and Bonner and Smith take this as a significant omission.[62] But obviously the defense would not need her testimony, since Euphiletus has taken the precaution of providing himself with several free witnesses; while the prosecution might hesitate to summon her, either because they could not expect her to testify against her master, or because no possible testimony of hers as to the events prior to the fatal evening could controvert the testimony of Euphiletus' eye-witnesses to the adultery.

Finally we have a brief account of a homicide trial in the oration *Against Neaera*.[63] Stephanus is said to have brought a charge of homicide against Apollodorus before the Palladium, a charge which the court did not sustain. In the conduct of his prosecution Stephanus procured some slaves to testify in support of the charge, but he produced them before the court not as slaves but as citizens of Cyrene. Bonner and Smith pertinently ask why, if slaves were competent witnesses, Stephanus pretended that they were freemen.[64] Lipsius considered this objection to be of such consequence that he modified his original view to the extent of saying that slaves were competent witnesses only before the Areopagus.[65] But it is hard to understand why slaves should be competent witnesses in cases of premeditated murder and not in other homicide cases; and Lipsius gives no reason. A better answer might be to explain Stephanus' procedure on the ground that though slaves were competent witnesses, the testimony of free men would be more likely to bring about a conviction; and that was what Stephanus was after. The risk he ran in pretending they were citizens of Cyrene does not seem to have been very great.

What conclusions can we draw from these cases? It is possible, as we have seen, to explain the lack of slave testimony in each of the recorded cases without discrediting Antiphon's statements about the

[62] II, 226. [63] Dem. LIX, 9 ff. [64] II, 228. [65] *Op. cit.* p. 873n.

competence of a slave witness. But it must be admitted that the necessity for so much explanation is disconcerting. On the other hand, the statement of Antiphon cannot be explained as merely an assertion of the slave's competence to give *μήνυσις* before a magistrate;[66] and this statement is so explicit that when backed by the corresponding provision in the Platonic legislation there seems to be a presumption on the side of its accuracy as a statement of Attic law. But it is also evident from the cases we have examined that the slave witness was not necessarily exempt from torture. The *πρόκλησις εἰς βάσανον* was allowed in murder trials as in others. Furthermore, it is probable that the prevailing prejudice in favor of the *βάσανος* for slaves would influence a litigant to resort to that procedure whenever possible, even though the law permitted an alternative procedure. And it is probably also true that slave testimony, though legally admissible, had very little weight with the judges. In short, the testimony of slaves was in all probability little used, and the principle of law which authorized it may have been in the fourth century merely a hallowed relic of ancient procedure. It is significant that Antiphon, who is our only authority for this principle, belongs to the late fifth century; whereas the case most difficult to explain—viz. Stephanus' prosecution of Apollodorus—occurred at least half a century later. This suggests that the principle was of more importance in the fifth than in the fourth century. If this be the situation, we can understand why Plato, with his preference for the ancestral laws, and his policy of making full use of slaves in the apprehension and punishment of wrong-doers, should have made this feature of Attic law so emphatic in his own legislation.

Even if this principle of Platonic law be taken as valid also in Attic law, we remain in ignorance about the scope of its application. Was any slave, male or female, competent to testify? Plato's law explicitly says *δούλῃ καὶ δούλῳ ἐξέστω* whereas Antiphon's text reads merely *ἔξεστι δούλῳ*. Was the slave witness competent to testify for either the prosecution or the defense, or only for the prosecution? Antiphon's words, severely taken, admit only the latter alternative, whereas Plato's law does not suggest any such restriction. Was the slave a compellable as well as a competent witness? The answer is "yes" for Plato's law,[67] but neither Antiphon's text nor the details of the cases he tells us about give the answer for Attic law.[68]

[66] See above, pp. 83 f.

[67] See above, pp. 79 f.

[68] Leisi (*op. cit.* p. 23) finds in Lysias IV, 10, 12, 13 evidence that the consent of the master was required for a slave to be a witness. But these passages seem to refer to *βάσανος*, not *μαρτυρία*.

Chapter VI

THE INHERITANCE OF SLAVE STATUS

Whenever the parentage is undisputed and the question at issue is which parent the child shall follow, if a slave woman lie with a slave or a free man or a freedman, in all cases the child shall belong to her master; if a free woman lie with a slave, the child shall belong to the slave's master; and if a slave woman lie with her own master, or a free woman with her own slave, and the fact be clearly known, then both the child and his mother, in the former case, and both the child and his father, in the latter case, shall be exiled to another land, at the command of the *nomophylakes* and the women in charge of marriage respectively (XI, 930d).

The fundamental principle of these provisions is clear. A child is regarded as free only if both parents are free; if either parent is a slave, the child takes the slave status. Let us compare this principle with the principle followed in other ancient systems of legislation.

A priori there are four possibilities with respect to the status of persons of mixed parentage. The child might be regarded as inheriting the status of the father, the status of the mother, the *melior condicio*, or the *deterior condicio*. Roman law seems to have decided for the second of these alternatives.[1] And this solution seems to have been widely prevalent elsewhere. Gaius calls it a principle of the *jus gentium* that *ex ancilla et libero servus nascitur, et contra ex libera et servo liber nascitur.*[2] Earlier it seems to have been a condition that the child of a free mother and a slave father should be free only if the mother was ignorant of the father's status,[3] but this condition seems to have been dropped in the classical Roman law. According to the Syrian law-book, which represents Hellenistic law of the Roman period, if the free woman goes to live in the house of the slave's master, or if she has been warned by the slave's master that her lover is a slave, then her children by the slave are slaves; otherwise, it seems to be assumed, the children are free.[4] The Graeco-Egyptian law of the papryi is similar: the child of a free woman by a slave is free, at least if the woman does not live with the slave.[5] This rule of residence is found also in the law of Gortyn. Here it is written that when the slave goes to the house of the free woman,

---

[1] "Die Regel des klassischen römischen Rechtes, dass zur Freiheit des Kindes Freiheit der Mutter auch nur in einem Augenblick nach der Konzeption genüge." Wenger, *Recht der Griechen und Römer* (in *Kultur der Gegenwart*), p. 186.

[2] *Institutes*, I, 82. Cf. Herodotus I, 173 (*ad finem*).

[3] *Ibid.* I, 86.

[4] Mitteis, *Reichrecht und Volksrecht*, pp. 365 ff.

[5] Taubenschlag, in *ZSS*, Rom. Abt. L (1930), 144.

the children are free; but if the free woman goes to the slave's house, the children are slaves.[6] A later decree of Gortyn declares categorically that the children of free mothers are free, which Kohler and Ziebarth interpret as abrogating the rule of residence laid down in the earlier law.[7] If this interpretation is correct, the law of Gortyn arrived eventually at the same principle accepted by the classical Roman law. As to the principle followed by Attic law, Dion Chrysostom tells us that the children of citizen mothers are free, regardless of the status of the father, and regardless of the mother's knowledge of the father's status.[8] This reflects primarily the law of the first century A.D., but we may take it, following Beauchet,[9] as probably valid also for previous centuries. The reference to the mother's knowledge of the father's status shows that the rule of residence was explicitly disregarded by Attic law, at least in the days of Dion Chrysostom.

Thus the principle that the child of a free woman is free seems to have been widely accepted, whether with or without conditions, in Greek and Hellenistic, as well as in Roman law. But there are also instances in Greek history of the sons of freemen by slave women being regarded as free. Thus Teucer seems to have been the son of Telamon by a captive slave woman.[10] Archelaus, king of Macedon, was born of a slave woman belonging to Alcetas, the brother of Perdiccas.[11] And in the story that Odysseus tells Eumaeus, he professes to be the son of a Cretan nobleman by a "purchased concubine," and yet to have inherited from his father like the other sons.[12] Such cases are difficult to interpret, since it may be that an act of emancipation and adoption had taken place. Since the power of emancipation usually lay with the master, we should expect that a father would often emancipate his natural son. But this explanation will not fit all the cases. At Sparta the Mothakes, or children of citizens and Helots, were ordinarily free, and often occupied important positions in the state.[13] Here if emancipation took place it must have been an official act of the state, not the private act of the father, since the private citizen had no right of manumission. Under these circumstances it may be as simple to conclude that Spartan law regarded such children as free by birth, not requiring emancipa-

---

[6] Col. VI, line 55 to Col. VII, line 5 (Bücheler-Zitelmann, p. 29).
[7] Kohler-Ziebarth, p. 52. [8] Dion Chrysostom XV, 446 R. [9] Beauchet, II, 406.
[10] Pauly-Wissowa, *s.v.* Teucros. [11] Plato *Gorgias* 471a.
[12] *Odyss.* XIV, 202–203. Megapenthes, son of Menelaus, was ἐκ δούλης; *Odyss.* IV, 12.
[13] Busolt, p. 667.

tion. And Kohler and Ziebarth interpret the law of Gortyn as implying that when a freeman begets children by a slave in his own household the children are free.[14] Thus it is possible that some Greek codes approached a recognition of the principle of the *melior condicio*, viz. that not only are the children of a free woman free, but also the children of a freeman (at least those by a slave in his own household).

However that may be, the principle of the *melior condicio* did not always hold at Athens. Demosthenes speaks of "concubines by whom free children may be had,"[15] which indicates that the children of free fathers were not always free, for there would have been no purpose in making this qualification if there did not exist *παλλακαί* whose children would be slaves. We may infer, then, that the children of slave *παλλακαί* would be slaves at Athens, those of *ξέναι παλλακαί* free. Beauchet nevertheless contends that in Attic law the child took the *melior condicio*, basing his contention upon the above-cited passage from Dion Chrysostom and a passage from Aristotle. Here Aristotle is discussing the qualifications for citizenship, and remarks that when there is a shortage of legitimate citizens a state may admit to citizenship persons born of a citizen mother and a non-citizen father, and even the children of a slave man or slave woman (the other parent, it is assumed, being a citizen). But when there is an adequate number of citizens, says Aristotle, the children of slaves are first excluded from citizenship, then those whose mothers only are citizens, so that at last citizenship is restricted to those whose parents are both citizens.[16] "We may conclude," says Beauchet, "that originally the child of a slave and a citizen possessed the rights of citizenship, and that later, when citizenship was denied him, he none the less preserved his free status."[17] But Beauchet's inference suffers from a double weakness. It rests upon the assumption that Aristotle, in the above passage, is comparing an earlier and a later stage of Athenian law, whereas he is really comparing the Athenian policy followed in times of emergency when new citizens are needed, with the policy followed when the supply of legitimate citizens is adequate. As a matter of historical fact we know that Athenian policy regarding admission to citizenship did fluctuate considerably between liberality and exclusiveness. The Athenians were generous of citizenship in the days of Cleisthenes,

[14] Kohler-Ziebarth, p. 52.
[15] Dem. XXIII, 55: *ἐπὶ παλλακῇ ἣν ἂν ἐπ' ἐλευθέροις παισὶν ἔχῃ.*
[16] Arist. *Pol.* 1278a 30 ff. [17] Beauchet, II, 407 ff.

exclusive in the days of Pericles, generous again as the Peloponnesian War depleted the stock of citizens, and again exclusive in the early fourth century.[18] Even though it should be granted that there was a general trend of Athenian policy from liberality to exclusiveness as regards citizenship, that would prove little with regard to the question of free or slave status. For Beauchet's conclusions suffer from the further weakness of assuming that in the cases in which the children of slaves were admitted to citizenship a previous or concurrent act of emancipation was not necessary. If emancipation was necessary, then it is clearly impossible to infer that a class of persons who might under exceptional circumstances be admitted to citizenship would in the absence of such grant of citizenship be regarded as free. The texts that refer to such grants of citizenship to slaves suggest that freedom was explicitly conferred at the same time.[19] The view of Hitzig[20] is therefore the sounder one, viz. that only in exceptional cases did Attic law regard the child of a slave woman as free (he suggests that if the father did not know the mother was a slave the child might be recognized as free); and that normally the child of a slave woman is a slave, whereas the child of a free woman is always free. In other words, Attic law normally followed the *juris gentium regula* of Gaius, interpreting it as did the classical Roman law; and when this principle was departed from, it was replaced by the more liberal principle of the *melior condicio*.[21]

When Plato's law is compared with other ancient legislation a striking fact emerges. The principle it employs for determining the status of persons of mixed parentage, viz. the *deterior condicio*, seems to be without parallel. The severity of this rule of law is mitigated somewhat by the provision for deporting the slave children born of the slave's master or mistress. Such children would ordinarily be born and brought up in the household of the free parent, and the close association between them and the free children of the same parent would be a source of cruel humiliation, as well as a dangerous source of discord. Deportation would probably, as Ritter remarks,[22]

[18] Kahrstedt, pp. 60 ff.; *Ledl*, "Das Attische Bürgerrecht und die Frauen," in *Wienerstudien* XXIX (1907), 173 ff.; XXX 1 ff,. 173 ff.; Müller, O., in *Jahrbuch für klassische Philologie*, Suppl. XXV (1899); Philippi, *Beiträge zu einer Geschichte des Attischen Bürgerrechts*, Berlin, 1870.

[19] Cf. Arist. *Pol.*, 1275b 37: [Cleisthenes] ἐφυλέτευσε δούλους; Lycurgus *Leocrates* 41: τὸν δῆμον ψηφισάμενον τοὺς μὲν δούλους ἐλευθέρους, τοὺς δὲ ξένους Ἀθηναίους κτλ.

[20] *ZSS*, Rom. Abt. XVIII (1897), 167.

[21] Becker's astonishing statement, that in Attic law the *deterior condicio* was the rule (*Platons Gesetze und das Griechische Familienrecht*, p. 70), professedly based on the above cited sources, is difficult to account for.

[22] P. 111.

amount to emancipation, though this would depend somewhat upon the law of the country to which the exiles went. In any case it would in the long run be an act of kindness to the child of mixed parentage to remove him from the humiliating conditions of life in the country of his birth. Plato's adoption of the principle of the *deterior condicio* is not difficult to explain. In the *Republic* Plato would have all unions regulated by the state so as to secure the perpetuation of the best stock and the prevention of deterioration among the guardian class (*Rep.* V, 459 ff.; cf. also *Rep.* III, 415b). Similar, though less drastic regulations regarding the marriage of citizens are advocated in the *Laws*, and their purpose is the same, to prevent the deterioration of the citizen stock. It is in this context that Plato's choice of the *deterior condicio* is to be understood; his purpose is to preserve the purity of the citizen body against any admixture with inferior stock. Elsewhere in the *Laws* he says that liaisons between citizens and slaves are to be discouraged, though he recognizes that the law can not entirely prevent them.[23] The law in question is, nevertheless, an attempt to guard against some of the evil consequences of such unions.

---

[23] VIII, 840 ff. The παλλακαὶ ὠνηταί of 841d shows that Plato is thinking of liaisons between citizens and slaves. In *Rep.* VI, 495e ff., Socrates expresses disapproval of unions between free women and freedmen; the offspring are bound to be bastards and beggars (νόθα καὶ φαῦλα). This shows that the principle of the *deterior condicio* which appears in Plato's *Laws* is grounded in conceptions he had entertained at least as early as the writing of the *Republic*.

Chapter VII

EMANCIPATION AND THE FREEDMAN

Two kinds of emancipation are recognized in Platonic law: emancipation by the state, and private emancipation.

Emancipation by the state occurs as a reward for certain services which the slave has performed: (a) for information (μήνυσις) of offenses against the law forbidding the appropriating of buried treasure (XI, 914a); (b) for information regarding neglect of parents (XI, 932d); and (c) for assisting a parent who is being attacked by his child (IX, 881c).

In the first two cases, Plato has merely taken over and adapted to his special purposes a familiar Athenian practice. We hear of emancipation at Athens for μήνυσις of treason, sacrilege, theft of public money, and violation of the ordinances respecting the importation of grain.[1] Emancipation for μήνυσις also occurs in the Graeco-Egyptian law of the papyri.[2] The principle therefore is a familiar one, though Plato's application of it varies somewhat from its historical parallels. No Greek state, so far as we know, used this device to ensure the sanctity of buried treasure, or to enforce the duties of children toward their parents; though knowing Plato's special preoccupations we can understand why he should have done so. No special importance, on the other hand, should be attached to the fact that Plato seems to make no use of emancipation to secure information of treason, sacrilege, and other offenses against the public. The two cases of μήνυσις mentioned above are not to be taken as exhausting the use Plato would make of this device. We have found that he gives a larger role to slave μήνυσις in the administration of justice than it had at Athens, and can hence safely infer that emancipation for slave μήνυσις would be correspondingly frequent. For the Greek slave the prospect of freedom was the most tempting reward that a legislator could offer, and we have already seen that it is Plato's resolute purpose to enlist the slaves in the enforcement of the laws.

In the third case, emancipation is a reward, not for μήνυσις of a wrong, but for active intervention to prevent a wrong. Plato's law would be a powerful inducement to the slave in a household to take

[1] Busolt, pp. 282, 982, 984; Lysias V, 5; VII, 16; Antiphon II, iii, 4; V, 34; Thuc. VI, 27, 2; *IG* II, 546.

[2] Taubenschlag, in *ZSS*, Rom. Abt. L (1930), 165.

the part of the parent if any strife should arise between him and his children, and would thus be a considerable support to that parental authority and prestige which Plato sets such store by. There is no known parallel to this in Greek law, for the maintenance of parental authority does not seem to have especially concerned the legislators of Greece. Yet again it is only the special application, and not the general principle of giving freedom for meritorious action, that is new.[3]

Plato's law makes no mention of emancipation as a reward for military service, though we hear of this frequently in Greek history.[4] But emancipation for this cause occurred only in times of crisis (if we except such cases as those of Dionysius and Agathocles), just as the use of slaves as soldiers was not a normal practice.[5] In Plato's state, as in the historical Greek states, slaves would not ordinarily be called upon for military service.

In general when the state emancipates a slave for any of the above reasons, Plato prescribes that the owner shall be compensated (XI, 914a, 932d), a principle which we know was followed in some Greek states, and probably also at Athens.[6] Plato provides, however, that if the slave belongs to the person benefited by his action, or to the person whose wrong-doing the slave's action exposes or prevents, no compensation is awarded (XI, 932d; cf. IX, 881c). And we should note the explicit injunction to the magistrates to see to it that no one injures the emancipated slave in revenge for his giving *μήνυσις* (XI, 932d). The equity as well as the utility of these provisions is so manifest that it must have been the intent, at least, of Athenian legislation to put them into effect.

In the cases thus far mentioned it is the state which confers freedom upon the slave; and though the slave may be privately owned, the consent of his master is not necessary for his emancipation.

---

[3] An interesting third-century inscription from Ilium provides that a slave who kills a tyrant shall be made a free man and a citizen. *OG.* No. 218.

[4] Thus the Athenians emancipated the slaves who fought at Arginusae (Aristoph. *Frogs*, 706 (*schol.*), 693–694), and there is a tradition that they did the same for the slaves who fought at Marathon (Paus. VII, 15, 7). After the battle of Chaeroneia a promise of freedom was made to slaves who would fight against Philip (Dion Chrys. XV, 21), and a similar promise was made at Aegospotami (Calderini, p. 170). Dionysius and Agathocles of Syracuse emancipated many slaves and enlisted them among their military forces (Diod. XIV, 58, 1; Justin XXII, 4, 5). At Sparta Helots were frequently given their freedom as reward for services in war (Thuc. IV, 26, 80; V, 34; VII, 58; Xen. *Hell.* VI, 5, 28; Plutarch *Cleomenes* 23); and Diodorus tells of a similar action at Rhodes in 306 B.C. (XX, 84, 3).

[5] Sargent, "The Use of Slaves by Athenians in Warfare," in *Class. Phil.* XXII (1937), 201 ff.

[6] Diod. XX, 84, 3; Busolt, pp. 289, 984.

Alongside this public emancipation, Platonic law also recognizes the right of the master to confer freedom upon his slave. The private character of this form of emancipation is clear, both from the repeated occurrence of the term "manumittor" (ὁ ἀπελευθερώσας) and from the special character of most of the provisions governing freedmen. Here again Plato's law embodies a practice familiar enough in the Greek states of his day. At Sparta, indeed, private emancipation was impossible, for the Helots were regarded as the property of the state and only the state could set them free.[7] But at Athens, and probably in all other Greek communities (save Crete and other places where serfdom existed) the right of a master to emancipate his slave was unquestioned and often exercised. The evidence indicates that manumission, while not unknown in previous periods, became common only in the fifth century.[8] Antiphon, writing in the late fifth century, tells us that it was the common practice to give freedom to slaves who had given information of murder.[9] This statement has sometimes been taken to refer to emancipation by the state, but as we have shown above, the μήνυσις of which Antiphon speaks here is not the strict μήνυσις of Athenian public law, but unofficial information leading to a private action against the murderer; so that the emancipation he refers to here is a reward conferred by the slave's owner, and his statement, though it may exaggerate the extent of the practice, shows at least that it existed. In the fourth century we find both Aristotle and Xenophon advising masters to hold out the prospect of liberty to their slaves as the best way of encouraging them to diligence and loyalty.[10] The wills of Plato, Aristotle, Theophrastus, Strato, and Lycon, all contain provisions emancipating certain of their slaves.[11] The inscriptions show that emancipation, both *inter vivos* and by testament, became increasingly common in later centuries.[12] It is tempting to attribute this increase to a growing feeling of discomfort among the Greeks with respect to the institution of slavery. But other factors must also have played their part, for the sums paid for freedom in later centuries were often higher than the purchase price of slaves, so that manumission was frequently a profitable transaction to the slaveowner.[13]

[7] Strabo VIII, 365; Paus. III, 21, 6; Busolt, p. 667.
[8] Calderini, *La Manomissione e la Condizione dei Liberti in Grecia*, pp. 3 ff.
[9] Antiphon II, iii, 4. [10] Arist. *Pol.* 1330a 33; Xen. *Econ.* V, 16.
[11] Diog. Laert. III, 43; V, 14–15, 55, 63, 72–73. [12] Calderini, pp. 32 ff. and *passim*.
[13] Zimmern, *The Greek Commonwealth*, p. 388.

In Plato's law manumission can apparently be effected by any slave-owner, whether citizen or *metic*.[14] No provision is laid down restricting the right to citizens, and furthermore the provisions we are shortly to examine regarding the status of the freedman rather suggest that Plato is thinking primarily of manumission by *metics*. For it seems to be taken for granted that the manumitted slave will fall into the *metic* class, that is, the class of free artisans; and since the slaves of citizens are forbidden to engage in trade or handicraft, the citizen's freedman does not fit so naturally into the picture. No restriction appears to be placed upon the right of an owner to emancipate his slaves, though in the case of citizens this right is implicitly limited by the general provision forbidding a citizen to alienate the equipment necessary for the maintenance of the lot. I have contended above that the agricultural slaves in Plato's state are not to be regarded as serfs: but it may have been Plato's intention that each lot-holder should have a certain minimum of agricultural laborers in his possession. The effect of this would be to limit the exercise of his right of emancipation, though not necessarily to create a class of serfs.

Plato's law is unfortunately silent on some points about which we would like to have information. Was publicity necessary to give effect to the will of the manumittor and to guarantee the status of the freedman? And if so, what form did this publicity take? There was no requirement of publicity at Athens or elsewhere until a later century;[15] but at Athens a manumittor would often make a public declaration in the law-court or at the festivals,[16] and elsewhere the act of manumission was often inscribed on a temple wall, or the freedman's name enrolled in a public register.[17] Would Plato's law permit a slave to purchase his freedom? Manumission in return for a cash payment by the slave was common in the fourth and later centuries. In such cases the slave was usually represented by a third party, sometimes a god, whose priests received the slave's money and therewith purchased his freedom. Or manumission could take the form of sale to a divinity, such as the Delphian Apollo, the intent of which was not to convey ownership, but to set the slave free.[18] There is no reference to

[14] This point is of some historical interest, since Calderini thinks that originally only citizens could effect manumission (p. 177). Manumission by a *metic* in relatively rare in the inscriptions. [15] Pauly-Wissowa, VII, 1 col. 96. [16] Beauchet, II, 473 ff.

[17] Calderini, pp. 125 ff. If Calderini's view of the *φιάλαι ἐξελευθερικαί* is correct (pp. 424 ff.) these constituted at Athens a public record of emancipation.

[18] Calderini, pp. 102 ff.

any of this in Plato's legislation. We may suppose that he would not look favorably upon manumission from mercenary motives, but there is no evidence of any attempt to prevent it. Again Plato makes no mention of testamentary manumission. The provisions of his law governing the relations of a freedman to his former master are obviously framed with a view to emancipation *inter vivos;* but since Plato himself made use of testamentary manumission, it can safely be supposed that he did not intend to exclude that type of manumission from his state, and the provisions of his freedman's law can easily be adapted to cover it.

The freedman occupies a distinct status under Platonic law. He is called ἀπελεύθερος,[19] ἀπελευθερωθείς, or ἀφεθείς, and is carefully distinguished from both the δοῦλος and the ἐλεύθερος. (cf. XI, 930d). The peculiarity of his status resides in the fact that he is still to a certain extent under the power of his former master; that is, he is obligated to perform certain services to his manumittor, and is subject to summary arrest if he fails in these duties.

A freedman also is subject to arrest [i.e. by his former master] if he fails to perform, or performs inadequately, the services (θεραπεία) he owes to him who set him free. These services shall consist in presenting himself thrice monthly at the house of his former master and offering himself for any honorable task within his power. Furthermore, as pertaining to marriage, he shall do always what seems good to his former master. A freedman shall not become richer than his master; any excess shall go to his master. The freedman shall not remain in the state more than twenty years, but like other resident aliens must depart at the end of that time taking his whole property with him, unless he obtains the consent of the state's authorities and his former master to remain. If a freedman, or any other resident alien, acquires more property than the amount possessed by a citizen of the third class, within thirty days from the day this excess appears he shall depart taking his possessions with him, and the authorities shall have no power to grant an extension of residence in his case. Whoever is seized and found guilty in court of violating this law shall be punished with death and his goods shall be confiscated by the state (XI, 915a–c).

It is clear that emancipation does not involve admission to citizenship. This is hardly to be expected under Platonic law, with its carefully selected citizen body; but in this respect Plato again is following ordinary Greek law. For neither at Athens nor in any other

[19] Calderini (p. 299) asserts that this term, as a special designation of the freedman, first appears in the epigraphical documents about the time of Plato. In the literature it appears earlier, e.g. in [Xen.] *Const. of Athens*, I, 10; Lysias VII, 10. The term ἐξελεύθερος, used indistinguishably from ἀπελεύθερος in the later literature, does not occur in Plato.

Greek city did emancipation carry citizenship with it. Admission to citizenship required a special act of the sovereign body in the state, whereas emancipation could be effected by the will of a private citizen. The Athenians did on rare occasion confer citizenship upon freedmen, but always by special act of the governing body.[20] And elsewhere we hear only rarely of freedmen being admitted to citizenship, and always by something like public action.[21] Thus we see that the admission of a slave or a freedman to citizenship was an unusual procedure in the Greek cities. At Athens it seems to have been the law that whoever proposed such a measure was liable to prosecution (i.e. to the γραφὴ παρανόμων) if anybody cared to raise the issue. Thus Thrasybulus, after the overthrow of the Thirty Tyrants, introduced a decree for conferring citizenship upon all those who came back from the Piraeus with him against the Oligarchs. For this he was later prosecuted by Archinus for having introduced an illegal proposal, on the ground that some of this number were clearly slaves; and this action of Archinus Aristotle calls "statesmanlike."[22] Dion Chrysostom refers to a "well-known law" at Athens according to which the "slave by nature" was ineligible to citizenship.[23] Whatever be the legal import of this phrase, it testifies to the exclusiveness of the Athenian citizen-body. The illiberality of Athenian law (and of Greek law generally) in this respect forms a striking contrast to the practice of the Romans, for at Rome (at least until the time of Augustus) emancipation involved admission to citizenship.[24] There is extant an instructive letter written by Philip V of Macedon about 219 B.C. to the inhabitants of Larissa advising them to grant citi-

[20] Clerc, *Les Métèques Athéniens*, pp. 221 ff. Aristotle (*Pol.* 1275b 36) tells us that Cleisthenes enrolled as citizens many of the resident aliens and slaves. After the battle of Arginusae both freedom and citizenship were conferred upon the slaves who fought on that occasion (Arist. *Frogs*, 693–694, 706, *schol.*). The famous fourth-century banker, Pasion, who began his career as a slave, became eventually a citizen by virtue of his services to the state; and the same good fortune befell his own slave Phormio (Dem. XLV, 24, 85; LIX, 2).

[21] At Ephesus sacred slaves, when emancipated, became citizens (Beauchet, II, 483; and Dareste, p. 24 §6). The Samians on one occasion, in order to enlarge the body of their citizens, conferred citizenship upon a number of their slaves in return for a payment of five staters each (Aristotle, Fr. 575, ed. Rose).

[22] Arist. *Const. of Athens* XL, 2.

[23] Dion Chrys. XV, 17.

[24] Cicero *Pro Balbo* 9 (cited by Mommsen, in *Hermes* XVII, 480n); *Sylloge*, No. 543, lines 30 ff. Beauchet calls attention to a curious mistake in Plautus' *Persa* (IV, iii, 474 ff.) resulting from this difference between Greek and Roman law. The author, with Roman law in mind, makes Dordalus, an Athenian who has just emancipated a female slave, speak as if he had made her a citizen.

Sumne probus, sum lepidus civis, qui Atticam
hodie civitatem
Maxumam majorem feci atque auxi civi femina.

zenship to all Thessalians and other Greeks living in the city. A later letter reproves them for not including freedmen in their grant of citizenship, and praises the liberality of the Romans in this respect.[25]

Under Plato's law, therefore, the freedman takes a position among the resident aliens or *metics*, not among the body of citizens. (a) Like the *metic*, the freedman can own property, but only property in movable goods; the right to own land is restricted to citizens.[26] This restriction reflects the spirit of Greek law, which invariably regarded the ownership of land as normally a prerogative of citizenship, though frequently, at Athens and elsewhere, the right to own land (ἔγκτησις γῆς) was conferred upon aliens by special act of the sovereign assembly.[27] In Plato's state such a grant of ἔγκτησις would be impossible, since all the land is held by citizens and they have no power to alienate their lots. (b) The freedman has the right to contract a legal marriage, though the consent of his former master is necessary. The reason his consent is required is probably to be found in the fact that, according to Attic law, the slave is regarded as a member of the family and his property normally reverts at death to his former master, not to any heirs of his own.[28] One of the legal consequences of marriage would be the recognition of heirs to the freedman's estate other than his former master. It is probable that in this requirement Plato is following Attic law, though we cannot be sure. (c) The freedman's term of residence in the state is limited to twenty years, as it is for the *metic*, unless the authorities specifically grant an extension of time. (d) Again, like the *metic*, the freedman can own only a limited amount of property. These last two restrictions upon the status of the freedman are doubtless Plato's own invention, since they are not to be found in any extant Greek law. The reasons for these restrictions cannot be adequately discussed without considering at length the entire institution of alien residence (μετοίκησις) in Platonic law and comparing it with current Greek practice. But it is evident that Plato desires, on the one hand, to avoid the Spartan extreme of excluding all aliens from the state, and on the other hand to prevent the state from being

[25] *Mitteilungen des Deutschen Archäologischen Instituts in Athen*, VII, 61; Mommsen, in *Hermes*, XVII, 467 ff.

[26] At the founding of the colony all the land, except that set apart for the gods, is to be divided into citizen-holdings, and these lots are to remain forever after in the possession of the heirs of the original lot-holders (V, 737e, 738d, 740b ff.).

[27] Szanto, *Das Griechische Bürgerrecht*, p. 7; *CIG* 90, 92; *CIA* II, 1, Nos. 4, 70, 186.

[28] Isaeus IV, 9; Arist. *Rhet. ad Alex.* 1422b 9f.

overrun by aliens who, by their numbers or wealth, might exert too powerful an influence upon the life of the citizens. It has been maintained that Plato's provisions are after all but a milder form of the Spartan policy of excluding aliens (ξενηλασία), since the two restrictions mentioned are such as to discourage the settlement of foreigners in his state.[29] But we must remember that the state has power to waive the restrictions regarding the term of residence in deserving cases; and perhaps the twenty-year period was intended by Plato to be a period of probation, permitting the state to select intelligently its permanent *metic* population. Furthermore, Plato levies no special tax upon *metics* and freedmen, as was customary in the Greek cities.[30]

The ownership of property implies some measure of legal capacity, and particularly the right of access to the courts. The question thus arises whether the freedman can bring suit and be sued in his own right, or whether he requires a freeman to represent him in his legal relations. We know that in Attic law every *metic* (and likewise every freedman) was required to have a προστάτης, or patron; but just what the functions of this προστάτης were has been a matter of prolonged controversy. Some have maintained that he represented his *metic* client in all his legal relations,[31] while others have regarded his sponsorship as limited to the act of enrolling the metic on the books of the deme, the *metic* thereafter being legally competent to bring action on his own account.[32] Now it is noteworthy that Plato makes no mention of a προστάτης in his legislation regarding *metics* and freedmen. Did he consider this requirement so obvious that it did not need explicit statement? Or are we to infer that the freedman and the *metic* have no need of a προστάτης in ordinary legal matters? We know from Harpocration and the inscriptions that in the Hellenistic period the freedman was generally required to choose his former master as his προστάτης.[33] But if we attribute to Plato the intention of imposing such a requirement we find that one of the emphatic provisions of the law above cited (XI, 915a–c) does not

---

[29] Hommel, in Pauly-Wissowa, XV, 2, 1456.

[30] Harpocration (*s.v.* μετοίκιον) asserts that every resident alien and freedman at Athens was required to pay a tax amounting to twelve drachmae a year for a man and six drachmae for a woman. This was by no means a nominal tax, for a drachma was regarded as a fair day's wage in the fourth century. Plato (VIII, 850a) explicitly says that no μετοίκιον nor any other tax is to be collected: "the only tax required is good conduct."

[31] Lipsius, pp. 370 ff., 791 ff.

[32] Clerc, *Les Métèques Athéniens*, pp. 261 ff.; Wilamowitz, in *Hermes* XXII (1887), 107 ff.

[33] Calderini, pp. 272 ff.; for Harpocration, see below, note 37.

make sense. The law requires that the freedman, in order to overstay his period of twenty years, must secure the consent, not only of the state officials, but also of his former master. Now if he was required to have a προστάτης to represent him in all legal relations, and if this προστάτης had to be his former master, then this special provision in the text would be pointless. For the freedman's appeal to the authorities for an extension of his residence would be presented through his former master, and the master's consent would *ipso facto* be manifest. To give any sense to this clause in the text we must assume either that the freedman was not required to have a προστάτης in all his legal relations, or that, although a προστάτης was necessary, it could be someone other than the former master. Since the relations between the freedman and his former master are in other respects so close under Platonic law, it hardly seems likely that Plato would permit the freedman to choose any other than his master if a προστάτης was required. We can only conclude, therefore, that if a προστάτης was required, his functions were limited; in other words, the freedman could sometimes take legal action on his own account.[34]

Thus far we have considered the respects in which the status of the freedman is identical with that of the *metic*. We must now direct our attention to the fact that in Platonic law, and also in common Greek law, the freedman was distinguished from the other *metics* by the relationship in which he stood to his former master, and the specific duties (θεραπεία) based upon this relation.

To get a background for understanding the θεραπεία of Platonic law, let us first look at the obligations of the freedman to his former master under Greek law. If we can judge of the law and the customs by the manumission documents brought together and exhaustively analyzed by Calderini, we must conclude that unconditional emancipation was exceedingly rare, if indeed it was possible under Greek law. The intent of the manumittor to confer freedom upon the slave is made manifest in the formula which recurs in hundreds of these in-

[34] Obviously the requirement that the freedman could act legally only through his προστάτης would be awkward as well as unjust, if the προστάτης was his former master. For under these conditions the freedman, as defendant in a δίκη ἀποστασίου would be represented in court by the prosecutor of the suit! (For this suit, see below, p. 104.) Consequently it seems necessary to conclude that the function of the προστάτης in Hellenistic law was a limited one. We simply cannot make sense of Harpocration's text if we assume that he represented his client in *all* litigation. Clerc and Wilamowitz are clearly right as against Lipsius (see above, notes 31, 32), at least for the law of the fourth and later centuries. It is possible that in earlier centuries the function of the προστάτης was much broader. See Kahrstedt, pp. 304 ff.

scriptions: the slave is "to be free and subject to no man's claim, to do what he will and to go where he will."[35] But in the vast majority of cases this nominally unconditioned freedom is restricted by special obligations laid upon the freedman, obligations which he is compelled to discharge at the risk of having his emancipation annulled. These obligations were of two main sorts, personal and financial.[36] The freedman could be required to live near his master and perform certain prescribed services for a period of time, perhaps until the death of the master; or perform these services for some third party designated by the master. And again a freedman might be obligated to pay a sum of money (distinct, of course, from whatever sum may have been paid at the time of manumission) at some prescribed future date to the manumittor or some other person designated by him. Harpocration also tells us that the freedman was obligated to select his former master as his *προστάτης* and perform certain other duties "which the law prescribes." The law also provided a special remedy for securing the discharge of these obligations, viz. the suit for apostasy (*δίκη ἀποστασίου*) which the manumittor could bring against his freedman for alleged breach of obligations. This suit had peculiar consequences: the convicted freedman lost his freedom entirely and reverted to the slave status, while if the charge was not sustained, the accused was acquitted of all further obligations toward his manumittor, and thus became completely free.[37]

These conditions often made the lot of the freedman a most onerous one, scarcely distinguishable, in some cases, from slavery itself. Not only was he often required to work as hard for his master after emancipation as before, but he was also under the constant threat of the *δίκη ἀποστασίου*, with the prospect of having his emancipation annulled and reverting in name as well as in fact to the slave status. In these features Greek law diverges sharply from the principle of Roman law, which recognized none but unconditional emancipation, at least *inter vivos*.[38] An individual once declared free could not be regarded as under an obligation to serve his manumittor; and according to Roman law, if a manumittor wished redress against a

[35] Calderini, p. 286: *ἐφ' ᾧτε ἐλεύθερος εἶμεν καὶ ἀνέφαπτος ἀπὸ πάντων, ποιέων ὅ κα θέλῃ καὶ ἀποτρέχων οἷς κα θέλῃ.* [36] Calderini, pp. 270 ff.

[37] Harpocration-Suidas: *ἀποστασίου· δίκη τίς ἐστι κατὰ τῶν ἀπελευθερωθέντων δεδομένη τοῖς ἀπελευθερώσασιν, ἐὰν ἀφιστῶνταί τε ἀπ' αὐτῶν ἢ ἕτερον ἐπιγράφωνται προστάτην, καὶ ἃ κελεύουσιν οἱ νόμοι μὴ ποιῶσιν.*

[38] Beauchet, II, 501; Wenger, *Recht der Griechen und Römer*, p. 190.

delinquent freedman he could proceed only by bringing an ordinary suit as against any other freeman, whereas the δίκη ἀποστασίου of Attic law clearly put the freedman at a legal disadvantage as compared with other freemen. Considering these circumstances, we are not surprised to find that the distinction between slave and freedman is often obscured in the Greek texts. Even in the fourth and later centuries, when ἀπελεύθερος had come into general use, we find the word δοῦλος frequently used where freedman is clearly meant.[39] The implication is that in Greek popular thought as well as in Greek law the distinction between slave and freeman was so sharply drawn that only in rare cases could emancipation erase it.

It is an interesting fact that in the earliest manumission inscriptions (those dating from the fifth and fourth centuries) there is no mention of these special obligations exacted of the freedman; whereas in the later inscriptions, especially from the second century onward, such conditions are usually present and stated with great precision. Are we to suppose that the practice of attaching conditions to emancipation was a development of the Hellenistic age and was foreign to the principles of Greek law in the classical period? It seems on *a priori* grounds improbable that such a striking and common feature of later Greek law should have come about otherwise than as a development of tendencies and practices of an earlier period. We can only believe, with Calderini, that in the earlier centuries the conditions of emancipation were usually specified orally, that it is only the practice of reducing these conditions to writing that arose later.[40] This change Calderini ascribes to the fact that manumission became more and more a financial transaction between master and slave, and to the relatively greater independence enjoyed by the freedman in later times. We know also that the δίκη ἀποστασίου existed as early as the late fifth or the early fourth century,[41] and since this was the remedy provided a manumittor for breach of obligations on the part of his freedman, there can be no question that such obligations were recognized by law at that time, however vaguely they may have been conceived.

The question arises to what extent these obligations of the freedman should be regarded as founded on public law. If we consider

[39] Cf. Dem. XXII, 61: δοῦλον ἔφη καὶ ἐκ δούλων εἶναι, καὶ προσήκειν αὐτῷ τὸ ἕκτον μέρος εἰσφέρειν μετὰ τῶν μετοίκων. Athenaeus (VI, 226b) cites Chrysippus to the effect that a freedman was still a δοῦλος but not an οἰκέτης. [40] Calderini, p. 271.

[41] Two of the lost orations of Lysias are concerned with δίκαι ἀποστασίου. Fragments 8 and 109 (Thalheim).

only the inscriptions of the later period we might be inclined to regard the obligations as created by the manumission agreement, in consequence of the master's right to dispose of his property on his own terms, and of the slave's right to take obligations on himself in return for freedom. For the utmost variety of personal services or financial payments is exhibited by these manumission acts, while there seems to be no obligation that cannot be waived if the manumittor chooses. Thus the requirement that the freedman must choose his former master as his *προστάτης* is explicitly waived in one inscription;[42] and in others the slave is expressly permitted to live where he pleases.[43] The very fact, however, that the manumittor expressly waives these conditions indicates that they would ordinarily be understood when not explicitly mentioned; in short, that there were certain generally recognized obligations to which a freedman could be held, even in the absence of any statement of these obligations in the manumission act. For the earlier period such an interpretation is inescapable; for as we have seen it was not at first customary to state conditions in the manumission acts, and yet the *δίκη ἀποστασίου* was in existence as a legal remedy at the disposal of a master against a delinquent freedman. Whether these generally understood obligations were ever precisely defined in written law may well be doubted; but there can be no doubt that Greek sentiment and Greek custom presumed that a freedman owed certain duties toward his former master, duties which, unless explicitly renounced by the manumittor, would be enforced by the courts. Only so can we understand the curious language of Harpocration who, after mentioning two specific duties whose violation would permit the use of the *δίκη ἀποστασίου*, adds: "and for otherwise failing to do what the laws prescribe."[44]

Thus the dispute between Clerc and Calderini as to whether the status of the freedman before the law was or was not identical with that of the *metic* comes to this: whether the special obligations imposed upon the freedman with respect to his former master, and the peculiar remedy provided by law to enforce these obligations (a remedy distinct in kind from those applicable to other private obligations), amount to giving a distinct legal status to the freedman. Clerc's assertion[45] that the obligations of freedmen toward

---

[42] Calderini, p. 272. [43] Calderini, p. 287.

[44] See above, note 37. Pollux (III, 83) says that Demosthenes speaks of *νόμοι ἀπελευθερικοί*. Such *νόμοι* must have dealt in part with the duties of the freedman to his former master.

[45] Clerc. p. 294.

their manumittors were of a private nature is true enough, but it should be added that they were presumed to hold whether or not they had been explicitly assumed by the freedman; and it should also be noted that the liability to the *δίκη ἀποστασίου* is a circumstance which, as Calderini maintains,[46] resulted in giving the freedman a more vulnerable legal status than that possessed by the *metic*.

Turning our attention now to Plato's law, we must first of all bear in mind that its provisions belong to a period considerably earlier than that to which the vast majority of the inscriptions studied by Calderini belong. At the time when Plato wrote it seems not to have been customary to make a precise record of the duties to be expected of the freedman after emancipation, although such duties were universally regarded as binding. This law is of considerable historical interest, therefore, as throwing some light on what was generally expected of the freedman in the fourth century; and Plato's relatively explicit formulation of these obligations is probably to be credited to him as an improvement upon the usual procedure of his day. The obligations Plato's law lays upon the freedman are the following: (a) he must appear thrice monthly at his former master's house and offer himself for any honorable service within his power; (b) he must not marry without the consent of his former master; (c) if he becomes richer than his former master, the excess must be given to the master; (d) his master's consent is required if he desires to stay in the country longer than the normal limit of twenty years after emancipation. These duties constitute what Plato calls the *θεραπεία* of the freedman to his master, a term which connotes not only service, or benefit, but also respect and worship.[47]

It is instructive to compare this list of duties with those found in Harpocration and the emancipation inscriptions. We have already noted the absence of any mention of a *προστάτης*, and have shown that even if it be assumed that Plato takes such a requirement for granted, it is evident that the freedman could sometimes take legal action on his own account.[48] Whether or not this represents a divergence from current Greek practice is doubtful. It is true that

---

[46] Calderini, p. 315.

[47] The term *θεραπεία* is explicitly applied only to the first two of the duties above mentioned, the last two being included under the more general regulations applicable to freedmen and *metics* alike, but there can be no doubt, I think, that of these more general regulations those involving obligations toward the master are intended to fall under *θεραπεία*.

[48] Above, p. 103.

Harpocration and the later inscriptions place great emphasis upon the requirement of a *προστάτης*,[49] but the point to be determined is the function of such a *προστάτης*. It seems to me incredible that the freedman and *metic* had to be represented in all their legal relations by a *προστάτης*, as Lipsius maintained. Such a view is incompatible with the texts and with principles of equity. The function of the *προστάτης* in Greek law must have been a limited one; and if so Plato's law shows no significant departure from current pactice. Again there is no requirement in Platonic law that the freedman must live near his former master; on the contrary, the first of the above obligations implies that a freedman might live apart from his master, perhaps at a considerable distance. Harpocration's statement that a suit for apostasy would lie against a freedman who had "left" his master (the *ἀφιστῶνται* of the text is the word sometimes used of runaway slaves) seems to imply that the freedman was supposed to remain near his master, perhaps in his household; and this requirement is sometimes made in the manumission inscriptions. Yet Calderini has shown that it was not a universal requirement, and that at Athens, in particular, the freedman often lived in a different deme from his master.[50] The omission of any mention of money payments in Plato's law is striking when compared with the manumission inscriptions of the later centuries;[51] but the practice of his own day was probably also much less mercenary than that revealed in the later inscriptions. Again in the inscriptions a term is usually set to the period during which the services of the freedman can be exacted: in the simplest cases the freedman is to serve during the lifetime of the manumittor, but a term of years may be specified, such as ten years, or even one year.[52] No such term is set in Plato's law; but its place is taken by the provision that limits the normal stay of a freedman after emancipation to twenty years. Departure from the country would of course terminate the freedman's obligations.

Plato's law includes some duties not found in the later documents.

---

[49] Calderini, pp. 272 ff.; Harpocration, as above, note 37.

[50] The Athenian *φιάλαι ἐξελευθερικαί* show the freedman living in a different deme from his former master. If Calderini's interpretation of these *φιάλαι* is correct, we must conclude that the freedman was not required to live near his manumittor in Plato's day (Calderini, pp. 424 ff.). A decree of Gortyn of the sixth century designates a special quarter of the city where the freedmen may live "if they wish." *IJG*, I, 403.

[51] Calderini, pp. 288 ff.

[52] Calderini, pp. 278 ff.

s in Attic law. For Plato apparently would not permit an owner
search of a runaway slave to enter the house of another without
householder's consent (XII, 954ab), whereas this seems to have
n allowed in Attic law.[5] It is to be noted that Plato makes no
ntion of a right of asylum for slaves, whereas this was a well-
wn feature of Attic and many other Greek codes.[6]
f no one disputes the ἄγειν, the claim of the person who has
le the arrest (the ἄγων) is apparently established. But any third
son who thinks the person being led into slavery (the ἀγόμενος)
freeman, is legally entitled to prevent the ἄγειν and secure a
cial determination of the issue. This is effected by the same
cedure as that provided in Attic law, viz. the ἀφαίρεσις (or
ρεῖσθαι) εἰς ἐλευθερίαν.[7] In Attic law the furnishing of security
place before the *polemarch*,[8] but we do not know how many
dsmen were required.[9] The giving of a formal guaranty before a
istrate is probably also the procedure intended in Plato's law.[10]
btless the ἀφαιρούμενος himself could be one of the bondsmen,
le to offer adequate security, as in Attic law.[11] It is to be noted
the ἀφαίρεσις could be effected by anyone who was able to
ide adequate security, and is not limited to the relatives or the
guardian of the arrested person.[12]
hat were the legal effects of the ἀφαίρεσις εἰς ἐλευθερίαν? That
hat were the legal effects of the arrested person's status is
d not of itself settle the issue of the arrested person's status is
from the requirement of the bondsmen. This requirement
tless served a double purpose. Besides assuring the magistrate
there was a show of justice in the claim of the ἀφαιρούμενος, it
nsured the return of the alleged slave to the ἄγων and the pay
of compensation for the loss of his services in case the cour
ed that the claim to ownership was justified.

n. LIX, 40; Thalheim, *loc. cit.*
υλία means immunity to συλᾶν or ἄγειν. For the right of asylum, see above, p. 55. F
meaning "punish" elsewhere in Platonic law, see IX, 868b, 879a.
texts sometimes use ἐξαίρεσις and ἐξαιρεῖσθαι in apparently the same sense as ἀφαίρε
ιρεῖσθαι. Lysias XXIII, 10, 12; Harpocration, *s.v.* ἐξαιρέσεως δίκη. For discussions
cedure in Attic law, see Lipsius pp. 639–642; Beauchet, II, 515–525; Partsch, *Bi*
cht, pp. 295–298. The classical sources are Lysias XXIII; Dem. LIX, 40, 45
, 62–66. Cf. also Dem. LVIII, 19–21; Isocr. XII, 97; Isaeus, Fr. 15, 16; Isocr. X
[8] Dem. LIX, 40; Isocr. XVII, 14. [9] Two only are mentioned in Aesch. I
Laws IX, 871e: the person accused of murder is required to produce three bonds
ole to ἡ τῶν περὶ ταῦτα δικαστῶν ἀρχή. Cf. also XI, 914cd, where the whole proce
f disputed ownership) takes place before officials.
n. LIX, 40, so interpreted by Lipsius, p. 640; also Isocr. XVII, 40.
ysias XXIII, 9, a brother is mentioned as a possible ἀφαιρούμενος; in Dem. LI
ρεσις is effected by Neaera's husband; in Aesch. I, 62, by Glaucon, who seems
on to the person released; in Isocr. XVII, 14 by a προστάτης. Cf. Isocr. XII,

Some of them, viz. (c) and (d), are closely connected with the peculiar institutions of Plato's state and we should not expect to find them elsewhere. So far as we know, it was not the practice of Greek cities to limit the wealth which a freedman could acquire, or to restrict his period of residence in the city. Certainly for the practice of Athens the career of the two fourth-century bankers, Pasion and Phormio, is conclusive evidence; both these men started as slaves, and both became very wealthy. These provisions of Plato's law are therefore distinctly less liberal than the practice of Athens. Plato's requirement that the consent of the manumittor is required for the marriage of a freedman is at variance with the later inscriptions, where the right of marriage is assumed and restrictions occur but rarely.[53] But Plato's law here may express a practice current in his century and later abandoned.

The most striking and important difference between Plato's legislation and Greek law is the remedy he provides for enforcing the freedman's obligations. Whereas the Attic law of his own and succeeding centuries permitted the manumittor to bring a δίκη ἀποστασίου against a delinquent freedman, Plato provides the same remedy as against a runaway slave, viz. summary arrest, the ἄγειν εἰς δουλείαν.[54] We may assume, I think, that this action may be countered by the intervention of a third party on behalf of the freedman, just as the ἄγειν in the case of an alleged runaway slave may be met by the ἀφαιρεῖσθαι εἰς ἐλευθερίαν. This is a fair assumption, since these provisions regarding freedmen follow immediately upon those respecting the ἀφαιρεῖσθαι εἰς ἐλευθερίαν. But even so, the substitution of the ἄγειν for the δίκη ἀποστασίου is anything but an improvement upon Greek procedure. However grievous it was for the freedman to be liable to the suit for apostasy, nevertheless it meant that any action against him had at least to go through the courts; whereas under Platonic law, even on the most liberal interpretation, a master's claim against his freedman would come to the courts only if the freedman could secure three responsible freemen who would interest themselves in his plight.[55] This provision would almost make the act of emancipation a meaningless form without any real effect upon the status of the slave. Plato's law here stands

[53] For the restrictions on the freedman's right of marriage that do occur in the inscriptions, see Calderini, p. 328. [54] See below, p. 111.
[55] For the procedure of the ἀφαίρεσις see the following chapter.

definitely upon a lower plane of legal development and of humanitarian sentiment than the law of Athens.[56]

In sum, we may say that Plato's law possesses the merit of having stated the obligations of the freedman more precisely than seems to have been the custom in his own century, and thus anticipates the development that took place in the Hellenistic age. But the obligations he imposes upon the freedman are seldom, if ever, lighter than those prescribed by current law and custom, and in some cases they are far more onerous than anything known at Athens. It is clear that he believes there is a vast gulf between the slave and the freeman, a gulf which emancipation cannot altogether bridge; and though this conviction was not peculiar to Plato but was deeply rooted in Greek consciousness and in Greek practice, yet in Plato's legislation it appears in an accentuated form. One is inclined to ask why, thinking as he did, Plato should have permitted emancipation at all in his state. For it is quite evident that Plato did not think that the slave was ordinarily qualified to assume the rights and obligations of a freeman. The attitude of the *Laws* is not the expression of a senile prejudice, for essentially the same sentiments are to be found in the *Republic*.[57] It seems fair to say that Plato permitted emancipation because it is sometimes advantageous for a master or for the state to offer slaves the prospect of freedom as an incentive to good conduct;[58] but that having permitted it, he was determined that it should be so defined and regulated as to differ but little in fact from the state of slavery.

[56] Meier's belief (*De bonis damnatorum*, p. 36) that Attic law permitted the ἄγειν in the case of delinquent freedmen is now generally abandoned. Beauchet, II, 503; Calderini, p. 333. Meier's view was based on a fragment of Isaeus preserved by Suidas, *s.v.* ἀνάκαιον :'Ερμοκράτη δὲ εἰς τὸ ἀνάκαιον ἐνέβαλε φάσκων ἀπελεύθερον εἶναι, καὶ οὐ πρότερον ἀφῆκε πρὶν λ' δραχμὰς ἐπράξατο. It is clear that Hermocrates' imprisonment was not the result of an ἄγειν εἰς δουλείαν, for if so he would have been under the power of his master, not in the city prison. His confinement must therefore have been incidental to some process in the courts, perhaps (as Beauchet suggests) a consequence of failure to furnish the surety required of all alien litigants in Athenian courts.

[57] We need only recall the bitter satire with which Socrates speaks of the "bald little tinker who has acquired some money and purchased his freedom and is now getting ready to marry his impoverished master's daughter" (*Rep.* VI, 495e) to realize the contempt Plato would ordinarily have for the slave who endeavored to rise above his station.

[58] Arist. *Econ.* 1344b 15 ff.

CHAPTER VIII

THE DETERMINATION OF DIS

Anyone in his right mind may arrest (ἀγέτω) h
him in any way he pleases within the bounds of w
arrest and secure a runaway slave belonging to on
If anyone demands the release (ἀφαιρῆται εἰς ἐλ
been seized as a slave, the man who has seized hir
but the releasor (ὁ ἀφαιρούμενος) shall furnish th
and only on these conditions shall the release ta
a release contrary to these conditions shall be li
(τῶν βιαίων), and if convicted shall pay the inju
twice the amount of damages claimed in the s
γραφέντος βλάβους) (XI, 914e).

This law begins with a technical legal te
denoted the act of taking summary possess
it implied a legally permissible exercise of
possessions of another. The word was als
denote any forcible arrest or seizure; hen
ἄγειν lies close to unlawful or violent captu
classes acts of ἄγειν καὶ φέρειν, whether c
sons or by public officials, as acts of vio
ὕβρις (X, 884a, 885a).[3] It is therefore not
ἄγειν of Greek law a primitive principle o
tamed and regulated in the interests of p
of the ἄγειν in Attic law was the ἄγειν
whereby a master both asserted ownersh
of his runaway slave, or of a person whor
slave. Several instances of the ἄγειν εἰς
ical texts.[4]

The important thing to note is that a
authorization to take possession of a pe
slave. How extensive was this right of ἄ
exercised not only by the owner of the s
or relative of the owner. This is not att
be an extension of Plato's own devising.
the ἄγειν in Platonic law would seem t

[1] Often used in the fuller form, ἄγειν καὶ φέρειν, w
nimals and persons. Cf. Thalheim, in Pauly-Wissow
[2] See Szanto, in Pauly-Wissowa, *s.v.* ἀσυλία.
[4] Aesch. I, 62; Dem. LIX, 40; Lysias XXIII, 9, 1

Plato's law tells us nothing about the subsequent steps in the judicial determination of the arrested person's status. The further provisions in his text deal only with a release unlawfully effected, that is, an ἀφαίρεσις effected by violence or subterfuge, without the giving of security. In such a case Plato prescribes that the ἀφαιρούμενος shall be liable to a suit for violence (βίαια) and if convicted shall pay double the damages claimed in the suit.[13] The extra damages are clearly something like a fine imposed as penalty for the unlawful act; but it is to be observed that Plato makes this fine payable to the prosecutor. Attic law also prescribed the δίκη βιαίων for unlawful ἀφαίρεσις and imposed a fine equivalent to the damages payable to the prosecutor; but it differed from Platonic law in making this fine payable to the state treasury.[14]

It is of some interest to inquire whether the ἀφαίρεσις could be used to effect the release of a *de facto* slave as well as to prevent the seizure of a person *de facto* free. There can scarcely be any doubt that Attic law provided a legal method of establishing the free status of a man unjustly held in bondage; but this is not to say that it permitted the ἀφαίρεσις in the sense just defined, for the peculiarity of this procedure was that it effected immediate release in advance of the judicial determination of the man's status. It is tempting to believe that Attic law permitted the ἀφαίρεσις in both types of cases, but there is no evidence justifying a positive assertion.[15] Nor can we make any positive assertion about Platonic law.

---

[13] Not "double the recorded value of the slave," as England translates. The use of βλάβους forbids this rendering; besides, elsewhere Plato uses ἀπογράφειν and ἀναγράφειν for the registering of property, not ἐπιγράφειν. For ἐπιγράφειν in the technical sense of setting down damages in a suit, see Liddell-Scott-Jones, *s.v.* III, 1.

[14] Lysias XXIII, 12; Dem. LVIII, 21. I take the μὴ δικαίως εἰς τὴν ἐλευθερίαν ἀφελέσθαι in Demosthenes' text to refer to an unlawful *aphaeresis*, as distinct from an adverse judicial decision as to the status of the person in dispute. Lipsius (p. 641, n. 18), I think erroneously, takes it in the latter sense. *Aphaeresis* did not always involve the payment of a fine, as is shown by Dem. LIX, 45 ff. And considerations of equity should make us sceptical whether a lawfully effected *aphaeresis* exposed the ἀφαιρούμενος to a punitive fine if the courts failed to sustain his contention that the man was free. The purpose of the *aphaeresis* was to secure a judicial determination of the man's status, and it would be enough to hold the ἀφαιρούμενος and his bondsmen responsible for actual damages caused the ἄγων through the delay in regaining possession of his slave.

[15] No conclusive inference can be drawn from Isocrates XII, 97: παραπλήσιον ἐποίησαν τοῖς παρὰ μὲν τῶν ἄλλων τοὺς οἰκέτας εἰς ἐλευθερίαν ἀφαιρουμένοις, σφίσι δ' αὐτοῖς δουλεύειν ἀναγκάζουσιν. Lipsius (p. 640, n. 13) indeed takes this passage as evidence that Attic law permitted the *aphaeresis* of *de facto* slaves; but is it certain that Isocrates is referring to legally effected and not to unlawful *aphaeresis?* Since the motives of the persons mentioned are questionable, the latter seems the more likely alternative. Besides, lawful *aphaeresis* required three bondsmen, whereas in the sort of case described by Isocrates the ἀφαιρούμενος seems to remain in undisputed possession of the slave, which suggests that he has acted alone, that is, he has merely taken possession of another's slave on the pretense of restoring him his freedom.

It is perhaps significant that Plato speaks of the ἀφαίρεσις only in connection with the ἄγειν εἰς δουλείαν. Elsewhere he mentions a right of ἀφαίρεσις vested in the owner of property that is in the possession of another (XI, 914d), but the analogy between regaining possession of one's property and effecting the release of a man unlawfully held in bondage is not exact enough for safe inference. Doubtless the γραφὴ ἀνδραποδισμοῦ, or prosecution for kidnapping, which he mentions elsewhere (XII, 955a; IX, 879a), could be used to bring about the eventual release of a man unlawfully enslaved. But whether or not the disputed person remained in bondage during the litigation we cannot say.

Assuming an ἀφαίρεσις to have been lawfully brought about, how would the main issue, viz. the disputed person's status, be judicially determined? As we have said, Plato's law tells us nothing about this stage of the proceedings. Nor can we pronounce with certainty upon the procedure employed in Attic law. The traditional view is that the person in dispute was regarded as devoid of legal capacity until the court had pronounced him free, and the litigation would therefore take place between the ἄγων and the ἀφαιρούμενος. The ἄγων could proceed by a δίκη ἀφαιρέσεως against the ἀφαιρούμενος, and if he won this suit, his ownership of the alleged slave was established, while the defendant was liable for damages. On the other hand, if the ἀφαίρεσις was sustained by the court, then the ἄγων was liable to a suit for violence (βίαια) or possibly ὕβρις.[16] But this view has been challenged by Partsch,[17] who contends that the disputed person could sue and be sued, and hence that the litigation took place between him and the ἄγων. According to Partsch the ἄγων would bring suit (a δίκη δουλείας) against the person whom he had arrested, the outcome of which would determine the man's status. The other party could if he liked bring suit against the ἄγων (what kind of suit Partsch does not say; probably a γραφὴ ὕβρεως or ἀνδραποδισμοῦ), and the decision of this likewise would constitute a determination of the question of status.

This type of action is obviously irregular and therefore affords no safe basis of inference as to what the law was. In fact it is hard to make sense of the passage at all, unless we assume that Isocrates is using language quite loosely. If we assumed that he is referring to lawful *aphaeresis* and referring accurately, then we must conclude that the *aphaeresis* of a *de facto* slave did not result in giving him freedom but only transferred possession from his former master to the ἀφαιρούμενος. This circumstance would make this type of *aphaeresis* quite different from the *aphaeresis* of a *de facto* freeman. Furthermore, it is hard to see any basis in equity or in utility for such an anomalous type of procedure.

[16] Lipsius, pp. 641–642; Beauchet, II, 518 ff.

[17] *Griechisches Bürgschaftsrecht*, pp. 295–298.

The difference between these two views is considerable, for it concerns the legal capacity of the disputed person during the contest over his status. The view of Lipsius and Beauchet has the advantage of resting upon a principle which we know was followed by Roman law, viz. that in a *causa liberalis* the person whose status was in dispute was an object of litigation, but not a party to it. But I have remarked before that we cannot be too vigilant against the danger of misinterpreting the concepts and procedures of Greek law by the use of Roman parallels. Some of the texts show that the disputed person possessed considerably more legal capacity during the litigation than the view of Lipsius would admit. The speaker in Lysias' *Pancleon* takes it as evidence of Pancleon's slave status that he allowed his companions to use violent methods in protecting him from an ἄγειν εἰς δουλείαν. For if he had been a freeman, asks the speaker, why would he have exposed his friends to prosecution for violence (i.e. for unlawful ἀφαίρεσις) when it was in his power to furnish bondsmen and by making a contest for his status get judgment against those who had attempted to seize him?[18] This shows not only that the disputed person furnished bondsmen before the magistrate (as Lipsius admits), but also that he could be a party to the litigation concerning his status and get a judgment against his opponents. A similar picture is presented by Aeschines' *Timarchus*.[19] Pittalacus, formerly a public slave, but later evidently a freedman living at Athens, had brought suit against Hegesander and Timarchus. Hegesander countered with an attempt to seize Pittalacus as a slave, but a certain Glaucon came forward and effected his release in a lawful manner. Hegesander then brought a δίκη δουλείας against Pittalacus.[20] The case was put in the hands of an arbitrator, whose partiality for Timarchus and Hegesander was suspected, for he delayed his decision again and again. Finally Pittalacus realized that his opponents were too much for him and offered to drop his suits against them if they would abandon their suit against him, and this was agreed to. It is possible, of course, that Pittalacus' suits against Hegesander and Timarchus could not be pushed as long as the δίκη δουλείας was pending; but if this is true, it is difficult to explain the bargaining power which Pittalacus evidently had. What is most telling, we hear nothing of a δίκη ἀφαιρέσεως against Glaucon, the ἀφαιρούμενος, but only of a δίκη δουλείας against Pittalacus. If

[18] Lysias XXIII, 12. [19] Aesch. I, 62–66.
[20] If the μαρτύριον is to be regarded as authentic.

we knew of only these two cases we should pronounce unquestionably in favor of Partsch's interpretation. But in Demosthenes' oration *Against Neaera* we have a woman who was seized as a slave by Phrynion, and lawfully released by Stephanus.[21] Phrynion brings suit against Stephanus, not against Neaera. It does not remove the difficulty to point out that Neaera was a woman, for suits were frequently brought against women in Attic law (the very oration from which this narrative is drawn is a case in point). Nor was the suit against Stephanus incidental to a separate suit against Neaera, for the arbitrators in the case of Stephanus passed on the question of Neaera's status as well as on Phrynion's claim for damages.[22] Thus it appears that under certain circumstances the litigation took place (as the traditional view asserts) between the ἄγων and the ἀφαιρούμενος, and that the outcome was binding upon the person in dispute, though he (or she) had not been a party to it.

These apparently conflicting data can be reconciled if we assume that an ἄγων had two lines of legal action open to him: either a δίκη δουλείας against the alleged slave, or a δίκη βλάβης (or ἀφαιρέσεως) against the ἀφαιρούμενος. In certain circumstances (e.g. when the disputed person was legally dependent on the ἀφαιρούμενος, as Neaera was upon Stephanus, or as any woman or minor would be upon a κύριος) the δίκη βλάβης would be preferable; for it would permit, not only the recovery of the slave, but also the collection of damages from the ἀφαιρούμενος. But the δίκη δουλείας would be necessary when, as in the case of Pittalacus, the person in dispute lived apart from the ἀφαιρούμενος and was legally competent to bring a counter suit. Under such circumstances he could resist a judgment rendered against the ἀφαιρούμενος, and it would be necessary to proceed against him directly; and an additional suit would be necessary to collect damages from the ἀφαιρούμενος. Thus Partsch's view needs to be slightly modified, but not with respect to his main contention. All the evidence goes to show that a person competent to sue at the time of arrest was competent to take legal action to protect his free status; in other words, that Attic law, unlike Roman law, allowed the person whose status was in dispute to become a party to the litigation if he was *de facto* free at the beginning of litigation. One may even look upon the ἀφαίρεσις εἰς ἐλευθερίαν as a device designed to set the arrested person at liberty in order that he might

---

[21] LIX, 40, 45. [22] LIX, 46.

exercise without hindrance his legal capacity to defend himself.

Can we assume that this is also the principle Plato intended to follow? Since Plato gives no details of the procedure subsequent to the ἀφαίρεσις, we can only reason from general considerations. In the details of the ἀφαίρεσις as given in Plato's law there is no noticeable departure from Attic law. Plato requires three bondsmen, whereas Attic law apparently was not so precise. Plato says that these bondsmen are to be furnished by the ἀφαιρούμενος, whereas Attic law allowed the person in dispute to furnish security. This second point was regarded by Lipsius as a significant divergence from Attic procedure.[23] But Attic law required the ἀφαιρούμενος to furnish security; that is, he was ultimately liable if security was not forthcoming to support the ἀφαίρεσις, and this is just what Plato's law says. Whether it was the person in dispute or the ἀφαιρούμενος who found these bondsmen does not seem to be a matter of legal importance. Since then there is no significant departure from Attic law with respect to the ἀφαίρεσις, we may presume that Plato also intended to follow Attic law with respect to the procedure subsequent to ἀφαίρεσις.[24] In this part of his legislation, as elsewhere, Plato seems to have chiefly in mind the prevention of violent methods of procedure; hence the careful delimitation of the right of ἄγειν, and the emphasis upon the distinction between lawful and unlawful ἀφαίρεσις.

The only other Greek code whose provisions regarding cases of contested status we know is the law of Gortyn; and fortunately that law is particularly well preserved on just this point.[25] This section begins with a prohibition of the use of the ἄγειν before the courts have passed judgment.[26] To understand just what this prohibition means, we need to distinguish carefully the three types of dispute which come under the provisions of the law: viz. (1) the suit to

---

[23] Lipsius, p. 641, n. 16.

[24] Certainly we cannot say that Plato's law regards the person in dispute as devoid of all legal capacity, as Partsch asserts (*Bürgschaftsrecht*, pp. 297–298). Since this astonishing interpretation is not supported in his text, I can explain it only by supposing that Partsch has erroneously taken Plato's law regarding unlawful *aphaeresis* to be a law covering the settlement of the question of status. To the suit for unlawful *aphaeresis* the person whose status is in dispute would of course not be a party; but that is not to say he would not be a party to the suit regarding his status. The two suits were distinct, the former being secondary and incidental to the latter.

[25] This section of the law covers the whole of the first column of the famous inscription discovered in 1884. For discussion and interpretation of this section, see Bücheler-Zitelmann, pp. 78–100; Partsch, *Bürgschaftsrecht*, pp. 296n, 298.

[26] Col. I, line 2: πρὸ δίκας μὲ ἄγεν. After decision has been rendered the ἄγειν is permitted (I, 55, II, 2). Even a magistrate is forbidden to make use of ἄγειν (I, 50–54).

establish ownership over a *de facto* freeman; (2) the suit to establish ownership over a slave in the possession of another person; and (3) the suit to establish the free status of a *de facto* slave. Since cases of the second sort do not involve any contest over status, they will not be further considered here. Now the ἄγειν prohibited in connection with the first type of suit is obviously the ἄγειν εἰς δουλείαν of Attic law; in other words, the law of Gortyn made judicial authorization necessary before a *de facto* freeman could be seized. This is a noticeable departure from Attic law, and shows that the law of Gortyn had gone much further than Athenian law in substituting legal process for methods of self-help. The prohibition of the ἄγειν εἰς δουλείαν made unnecessary any such procedure as the ἀφαίρεσις εἰς ἐλευθερίαν of Attic law; since a freeman could not be lawfully seized, he needed no one to effect his legal release pending the decision of his status. Hence the Gortynian code makes no mention of ἀφαίρεσις or of any procedure corresponding to it. Let us turn now to the third type of case, where the status of a *de facto* slave is under dispute. The ἄγειν prohibited here is the arbitrary and violent release or rescue of a person held in bondage.[27] Since the ἄγειν is prohibited in such cases, and there is no mention of any lawful method of effecting the release of a person held in bondage until the courts have passed on his status, we must conclude that a *de facto* slave whose status was in dispute must remain in bondage during the litigation, just as the *de facto* freeman remained free. In short, the law of Gortyn prescribes that the disputed person shall retain the *status quo* until a decision of the court is reached. And this, as we have argued above, is probably also the principle aimed at by Attic law.

Whether the law of Gortyn regarded the disputed person as a party to the suit or merely as an object of litigation cannot be definitely made out. A plausible case can be built up for the first alternative when it is a *de facto* freeman whose status is in dispute.[28] But since these three types of suits are treated as similar, and the person in dispute is certainly not a litigant in suits of the second type and probably not in suits of the third type, there is a strong presumption that in all these cases the person in dispute must be represented by

---

[27] This is the sort of release referred to by Isocr. XII, 97, if my interpretation (see p. 113, above) of this passage is correct. The provisions of the law of Gortyn confirm the view above expressed. [28] Partsch, *Bürgschaftsrecht*, p. 296n.

a third party.[29] The truth is, the text of the law is too lapidary to enable us to decide between these alternatives. The essential humanity of the law of Gortyn is, however, evident in the clause prescribing that when the witnesses disagree, some asserting that the man is free, others that he is a slave, the witnesses for his free status shall be given greater credence.[30]

---

[29] This is the view of Zitelmann (Bücheler-Zitelmann, p. 86).

[30] Col. I, lines 14–17 (Bücheler-Zitelmann, p. 17). Beauchet (II, 519) quotes as a parallel the Roman law: *Sed si et testes non dispari numero tam pro libertate quam contra libertatem dixerint, pro libertate pronuntiandum saepe constitutum est.* Digest, *De Manumissione*, XL, 1.

Chapter IX

SUMMARY AND CONCLUSION

The foregoing pages have made it clear that the slave under Platonic law had an ambiguous status: he was both a possession and a rudimentary legal person. Both these aspects of the slave must be kept before the mind if we are to see Plato's law of slavery without distortion. A portion of Plato's law considers the slave as a possession, and this part of the law is only a part of the more general law of property. Here belong the provisions entitling a slave-owner to compensation for injury done his slave property; and equally important, making the owner liable (within limits) for injuries or damages done by his slaves. And as a piece of private property, the slave is at the disposal of his master, who can sell or manumit, or use the slave for any purpose he pleases, subject to the restriction on occupations imposed upon citizens and their slaves, and subject also to the right of the state to make use of slaves on occasion for public works, and to emancipate a slave for services to the state. All this falls easily under the general principles of the law of property, though slave law is complicated by the fact that the slave is a difficult possession to manage, since he is able to act not only on his own initiative (like other animate possessions), but also with duplicity and cunning; and special provisions are needed to define the nature and extent of the master's responsibility for the actions of such an intractable kind of property. The point to be noted in this part of Plato's slave law is the respect paid to the principle of private ownership. Slaves are the property of their masters, not of the state (except for the negligible group of public slaves). When the state emancipates a slave for public services, the master is compensated, and possibly also when it makes use of slaves in the construction of public works, though this is more probably to be looked upon as a tax which the citizen wealthy enough to own slaves may properly be asked to pay. The intention of Plato's law to recognize and to give full protection to private property in slaves is beyond question. But the slave is not merely a possession; he is also, in a sense, a legal person, though his legal personality is in most cases quite rudimentary. The personality of the slave is evident in the fact that he is, on the one hand, subject to law and is held responsible in his own right for offenses; and on the other hand, the law affords him some protection in his own right and on rare occasions permits him to exercise something like active legal capacity. Even in his relation to his master the slave is considered as a subject, not merely as a possession: and the master is not merely his owner, but his lord, or ruler. The state with its law interferes but rarely with the master's rule over his slaves, so that the protection it gives the slave's person or possessions against his own master is exceedingly limited. Nevertheless, where the law of the state stops short, religious law with its sanctions takes the slave under its protection, at the same time imposing on the slave, as on any freeman, the obligations of "holiness." The recognition of the slave as a member of the religious community we found to be the most striking, as it is probably the most ancient feature of this part of Plato's slave law; and the distinctive character of this religious law of holiness, whose provisions are interpreted by a body of *Exegetes* connected with Delphi rather than with the political organs of the state, is clearly marked in Plato's legislation.

Though the slave is regarded as in some sense participating in the law of the city, his standing before that law is quite different from that of the freeman.[1] Like a freeman he is held responsible for offenses, and sometimes appears as a defendant in court. When accused of homicide it seems that he is entitled to trial. But his status differs from that of the freeman in that (a) the freeman is normally subject to punishment only by the public officials, whereas the slave may be punished by any free person; and (b) the slave is punished in his body, i.e. by stripes or branding, whereas fines and dishonor are prescribed for the freeman, his person ordinarily being immune. As regards the protection of his person and possessions, the slave's position before the law is hardly to be compared with that of the freeman. The law of the city does not specify what constitutes justice in the relation of masters to slaves, nor does it contain any remedies which could be used by the slave for his own protection against his master. Against another freeman the slave is protected by his master's interest in him, and by the remedies of the law which the master can invoke to protect that interest. Since the master can institute a charge of homicide, as well as a suit for damages, on behalf of a murdered slave, it is clear that the city's law is far from considering the slave as merely property, even though the protection

[1] Cf. IV, 718a and V, 730b where slaves are not included in the list of persons whose rights the laws should state.

it gives his person is casual and elementary. Only in one case does the city's law provide for the prosecution of a slave's murderer by persons other than his master, and that is when the slave has been murdered to prevent his giving information of unlawful acts. In this case the law provides that the murderer shall be prosecuted and punished as if he had killed a citizen. Obviously the purpose of this law is to protect the slave not so much in his own person as in his capacity as a public agent, a denouncer.

Only in rare cases does the slave enjoy anything like active legal capacity. The case just mentioned is one; when the slave has knowledge of certain criminal acts he has the right, as well as the duty, of laying this information before a public magistrate. By this means the slave becomes an agency in initiating the prosecution of offenders. The offenses enumerated of which the slave is allowed to give *μήνυσις* are offenses against the public or against the authority of parents. It does not appear that this right of *μήνυσις* includes the right to denounce his own master for cruelty. In the exercise of this right of denunciation the slave is protected (such at least is the intention of the law) against injury; and to induce slaves to give information, there are tempting rewards (e.g. emancipation) for denunciation, and severe penalties for failing to denounce. Besides the right of denunciation, Platonic law also gives the slave the right to testify in court like a freeman in a trial for murder, and even to act as *συνήγορος* in such cases.

But except in his public capacity, the slave has no rights of legal action. Though it appears that he can own property, yet it is very doubtful whether he can take legal steps to protect his "ownership." For the protection of this and all his other purely private interests he seems to be dependent entirely upon his master or some other person acting for his master. In this respect he is, as compared with freemen, outside the law. Both citizen and *metic* possess the right to take legal action to protect their private interests; both enjoy, not only the protection of religious and moral law, but also the protection of the city's courts. The citizen, of course, possesses more legal capacity than the *metic;* besides his political privileges, which the *metic* does not possess, he can initiate certain types of public prosecution that do not lie within the competence of the *metic*. But *metics* as well as citizens are "sharers in the law," whereas the slave, so far as his private interests are concerned, is without access to the courts.

Thus, though it appears that the slave is a person, he is a person subject in the main to the private authority of his master and without redress against the abuse of that authority. His master's will is the law he must obey. His status is that of an immature person, and his relation to his master is analogous to that of the child to his parents or elders. This analogy appears in many of the provisions of Plato's legislation.[2] But whereas the child's dependent status is temporary only, the slave's status is one of permanent legal immaturity. Even after emancipation he is still under obligation to his former master, and for failure (or alleged failure) to perform his obligations he may be summarily arrested by his master and reduced to his former condition of servitude, without being able to take legal steps to defend himself. Thus manumission does not confer full freedom; it does not sever the relation between master and slave; it leads, at best, to a milder and less manifest form of servitude.

Plato's law of slavery is no creation of his philosophical imagination. It is an adaptation of positive Greek law, and more particularly of the law of Athens. Again and again we have had occasion to notice, in the preceding pages, the correspondences and similarities between details of his law and the provisions of Attic law. Some of the more important of these correspondences may well be recalled to mind here: the nature and degree of the responsibility of masters for the offenses of their slaves; the application to the slave and to offenders against slaves of the ceremonial requirements of the homicide laws; the recognition of the slave's passive legal capacity, i.e. his right to act as defendant at law; the recognition of slave property, and of the slave's right to denounce offenses against the public, and to testify in murder cases. Plato follows Attic law in permitting manumission at the will of the slave's master; in the types of emancipation recognized and the requirement of θεραπεία from the freedman; in the sharp distinction drawn between the penalties prescribed for freemen and those prescribed for slaves. Terms like μήνυσις, μαρτυρία, ἄγειν, and procedures like the ἀφαίρεσις are taken

[2] Like the child he must be sternly disciplined (VII, 793e). He is not allowed to drink wine (II, 674a; cf. 666a). His testimony, like the child's, is acceptable in court only in murder cases (XI, 937ab). He may be punished on occasion by any free man over thirty years of age (XI, 914b), just as the child, who is in a sense a slave (ὡς δοῦλον) is to be punished by any free man who sees him doing wrong (VII, 808e). The criminal law abounds in such analogies. The slave who strikes a free man is dealt with like the youth who strikes an elder (IX, 882a); the slave who wounds his master like the child who wounds his father (X, 887b); and the slave who kills a freeman in self-defense like the child who murders his father (IX, 869d). Such analogies are most revealing as to Plato's conception of the legal and moral status of the slave.

over bodily from Attic law and used in their precise technical sense. On some of these points we have seen that Plato's law represents not only Attic law, but also principles and procedures widely prevalent in Greece, though our knowledge of non-Athenian Greek law is so fragmentary that it is very often impossible to make a proper comparison. This agreement with Attic law is so striking and thoroughgoing that we have not hesitated, on occasion, to use the Platonic provisions as decisive for Attic law where our other evidence alone does not produce full conviction. The legislation of the *Laws* (if this portion of it is not a curious exception to the whole) is the work of a man who had a competent knowledge of Attic law and legal concepts, and made generous use of this positive material in his own ideal legislation.

Of special interest is the agreement between the general character of the slave class in Plato's state with the corresponding class at Athens. The slaves in Plato's state are in general privately owned, though there are a few public slaves; they are of different non-Greek stocks, and their number is small compared with the total population of the state. In all these respects Plato's ideal state is a copy of his native city. What we know to have been the peculiar features of the Lacedaemonian form of slavery, viz. the vast numerical superiority of the slave population to the free, the institution of serfdom, the principle that the slaves belonged to the state primarily and not to the individual, the institution of the κρυπτεία or secret police to anticipate and prevent revolts among the slave class—none of these finds a place in Plato's law. This fact is significant in view of the common opinion that Plato's political ideals were much influenced by his admiration for Sparta and Spartan institutions. Unless his law of slavery is a strange exception to the rest of his legislation, this opinion would seem to need some revision. The foundation and substance of Plato's slave law is the law of Athens.

But Plato does not uniformly adhere to the Athenian law and practice of his day. We have noticed in the preceding pages many points on which Platonic law departs from its Athenian model, some of them trivial, but others of considerable importance as affecting the status of the slave. These departures from Athenian law are of particular interest as throwing light upon the direction of Plato's reforming tendencies.

In the first place, Plato is distinctly less liberal with regard to the status of persons of mixed descent. Attic law of the fifth and fourth centuries generally followed the principle that the children of free mothers were to be regarded as free, a principle which was followed by Roman law and which, according to Gaius, was a part of the *jus gentium*. There is reason to believe that on occasion Attic law was even more liberal and regarded the children of free fathers as also free. But Plato's law adopts the principle of the *deterior condicio:* a child born of one slave parent and one free parent inherits the status of the slave parent. This is distinctly more severe than Attic law; it is severer, in fact, than any slave legislation we know of in classical antiquity.

Secondly, although Plato's law permits manumission, as did Attic law, yet the status of the freedman in Plato's state is legally inferior to his status under Attic law. He is required, as in Attic law, to perform certain services for his former master; but whereas in Attic law a freedman who was negligent in the performance of these obligations was subject to a suit for apostasy, Plato permits the simpler and more summary remedy of the ἄγειν. This was the procedure used in arresting a runaway slave, and its legal effect was that a person so arrested could take no legal steps to vindicate his rights, but had to depend upon some third party to take action in his behalf. In the Athenian suit for apostasy the freedman remained in possession of his legal capacity. The substitution of the ἄγειν for the suit for apostasy is therefore decidedly prejudicial to the freedman and makes his status even more vulnerable than it was under Attic law.

Thirdly, there is in Platonic law an unmistakable tendency toward greater severity in the punishment of slaves. It was a common principle of Greek law, as has been shown above, that the slave should be punished with stripes, whereas the freeman's person was usually immune. Platonic and Attic law both accept this principle. But Athenian law had certain humane features that set it considerably above the law of other Greek states, so far as we can judge. Thus at Athens the number of stripes to be dealt the slave was prescribed by law, and was equal to the number of drachmae to be paid by the freeman. Plato's law hardly measures up to Attic standards in this respect. Sometimes the number of stripes is not fixed, and where it is specified, it often seems out of all proportion to the Athenian principle of one stripe to one drachma. Furthermore, if the statement of the Old Oligarch that at Athens it was forbidden to strike a slave has any foundation in fact, it must mean at least that the punishment of slaves for offenses against the law and for injuries to the person of freemen (not their masters) was the function of the public magistrates, not of the private person. Plato's law, however, not only permits an injured person to take summary vengeance upon a slave who has insulted or injured him, but even prescribes that freemen shall chastise slaves for certain offenses against the laws. This principle that any freeman is to be considered a magistrate authorized to administer punishment to a slave offender would naturally result in greater severity. Lastly, it was a principle of Attic law that a slave guilty of murder, even if the victim be his own master, must be delivered to the public authorities who alone were empowered to execute sentence upon him. But Platonic law provides that a slave who kills his master in anger is to be delivered to the relatives of the victim, who may punish him as they will, but the punishment must not be less than death. Even when, in another law, it is prescribed that the sentence is to be executed by the public executioner, the official is under the direction of the dead man's relatives, who are to determine how severely the slave is to be flogged before being put to death. These portions of Plato's law do not make pleasant reading. Attic law had long got beyond the principle of private vengeance in allowing the injured party or his representative to inflict the penalty for homicide, and in this respect Plato's law is a decided anachronism in the fourth century.

Lastly, certain omissions in Plato's law take on significance when considered with reference to the foregoing principles. Attic law, as we know, provided the remedy of a public prosecution against a person guilty of *hybris* toward a slave. Plato's law does not mention the γραφὴ ὕβρεως at all, and in the passage where *hybris* toward slaves is forbidden, it is clear that Plato is laying down a moral principle, not a rule of law to be enforced in the courts. Nowhere does Platonic law make any provision for the prosecution of the murderer of a slave except in the case of a slave informer who has been done away with by a guilty man who fears exposure. Again, Attic law recognized the slave's right to asylum in certain temples and holy places, where, if the priest permitted it, the slave could be safe from a cruel master. This was doubtless the most important means open to the Athenian slave to protect himself against bodily injury or death, for it was the one remedy which he himself could invoke. But the right of asylum is nowhere mentioned in Platonic law. Even if these omissions are accidental, they are at least an indication that Plato was not deeply concerned about the legal protection of the slave; and taken in connection with the innovations above mentioned we may easily suspect that their omission is not accidental.

For there is a common tendency in all these innovations of Plato. Their effect, on the one hand, is to give greater authority to masters in the exercise of rule over slaves, and on the other hand to accentuate the distinction between slave and freeman. The use of the ἄγειν against delinquent freedmen makes the status of the freedman more akin to slavery than freedom. The differential penalties prescribed for slave offenders, coupled with the peculiar Platonic prescriptions for applying them, and the lack of explicit legal remedies for the protection of the slave's person, all emphasize the fact that the city's law is in general for the protection of the freeman, not the slave. And the principle of the *deterior condicio* means that the slightest admixture of slave blood suffices to make one a slave before the law. To the same effect is the provision that slaves are to be of different nationality from one another and from their masters, and the moral injunction that masters should avoid all familiarity or intimacy with their slaves. We can only conclude that Plato's law represents a deliberate effort to sharpen the familiar distinction between slave and freeman, and to maintain it more rigorously than was done in Attic law and custom. This is confirmed by the fact that Plato's law nowhere prescribes sale into slavery as a penalty for offenses against the laws. This penalty frequently occurs in Attic law and elsewhere in Greece. Likewise man-hunting and piracy, two considerable causes of the enslavement of freemen in ancient times, are strictly forbidden. The freeman in Plato's state need never fear that he would lose his free status: once free, always free. But the recognition of this principle by Platonic law emphasizes even more the distinction between slave and freeman, and brings out more clearly the permanent inferiority of the slave's condition.

There are indeed certain respects in which Plato gives the slave a slightly better position before the law than he enjoyed at Athens. We have seen that Plato makes use of slave denunciation, a practice familiar at Athens, even going beyond Attic law in enlarging the number of crimes for which slave denunciation is permitted, and (what is more significant) he makes denunciation a duty of the slave, not merely a privilege. This indicates Plato's recognition of the slaves as important aids to the enforcement of the laws, and his deliberate effort to make more use of them in this respect than was done by Attic law. To the same end is his provision permitting the slave to act as *synegoros* in a prosecution for murder, and the admission of slave testimony without torture in murder cases (if these are departures from Attic law). To protect the slave informer, Plato provides that anyone who murders a slave for fear that he will lay information before a magistrate is to be punished as if he had murdered a freeman. And there are other provisions enjoining the magistrates to see that no one does injury to a slave informer. In all these respects the slave enjoys a larger measure of legal capacity and of legal protection than he did at Athens; but it is to be noted that these provisions affect the slave in what might be called his public capacity, i.e. as an instrument in the enforcement of the laws. We go astray if we look upon them as aimed at the protection of the slave's person in its own right, or as more than exceptions (justified on grounds of public policy) to the more severe principles elsewhere adhered to.

What is the source of these Platonic innovations? There is no known parallel elsewhere in Greece to Plato's adoption of the *deterior condicio*. Even the Spartans, whose treatment of slaves was noted for its severity, did not go so far as this. Plato cannot be looking to the institutions of early Greece, for we have abundant evidence that in earlier times descent from a slave did not disqualify for the position of a freeman. It is possible that this principle in Plato's legislation is without precedent in Greek law. In any case, it is to be taken as an expression of a belief in the natural inferiority of some kinds of human stock and a desire to preserve the purity of the free classes in his state. Since the slaves in Plato's state are non-Hellenic, this belief and this desire are not difficult to understand. It may seem strange, however, that Plato, holding these views, placed no restriction on manumission. The explanation is that manumission does not really effect freedom, but only an attenuated and disguised form of servitude; besides, the freedman's term of residence in the state is limited.

As to the other parts of Plato's innovations, I think we can say that Plato is looking, not to some other state than Athens, but to the Athens of an older time. The longing for the ways of the fathers, the *πάτριοι νόμοι*, is evident in many of the other institutions of the *Laws*. It is evident in the fundamentally agrarian nature of the economy Plato would set up; in the attention he gives to the organization of religion, and the emphasis upon simplicity, in art, education, recreation; and in the choice of a site for his city away from the seacoast and thus apart from the temptations of a maritime and commercial career, which he believes had been the ruin of Athens. Likewise in the authority he assigns to the master of the household we can recognize an attempt to revive the practices of an older Attica, when the patriarchal principle was more influential than it was in the Periclean and post-Periclean ages. As affects the slave, there can be no question that the power of the master was legally less restricted in the pre-Solonian period than afterwards. The protection which Attic law came to accord the slave, slight and inadequate though it was, is the result of the reforms of Solon and the commercial and industrial democracy which they made possible. Looking for his ideal in the pre-industrial and pre-democratic Athens, Plato naturally reinstates the master's authority and the sharp class distinctions of the earlier centuries. But to judge Plato's proposals aright we must bear in mind that though in pre-Solonian Attica there were fewer legal restrictions on the master's power, it is possible that there was also less abuse of this power by masters. When most of the slaves were of Greek blood and their relation to their masters' families was more durable, continuing from one generation to another, there were intimate personal ties to influence the sentiments of masters and regulate their conduct toward slaves. We know also that powerful religious emotions and practices were at work for the protection of the slave, a feature of the earlier age which reappears in Plato's laws. In the later centuries, with the decline of the religious sentiments, the growth of commerce and industry, and the importation of barbarian slaves, the relations between master and slave became less personal and sentimental. The slave tended to become chiefly an instrument of production and commerce, a valuable kind of property with a ready sale. The paradoxical nature of Plato's proposals is that he would reinstate the despotic authority of the earlier period without, however, reinstating the other conditions of that period that mitigated the despotism. For he copies the Athens of his day in thinking of his slaves as of non-Hellenic stock and without permanent connection with their masters or with the state. Thus he sets up the conditions that make legislation for the protection of the slave necessary, while ignoring the attempts of Attic legislation to furnish such protection.

It has been maintained that Plato at heart disapproved of slavery and in introducing it into the *Laws* was simply accommodating himself to his age.[3] This view is not likely to seem plausible to one who has considered carefully the materials presented in the preceding pages. One can think of numerous improvements that Plato might have made upon Attic law if he had desired to moderate the severity of an unnatural institution. The slave's power of legal action to protect his person or property might have been increased; or emancipation encouraged, or the status of the freedman improved by the abolition of θεραπεία. But instead, when Plato departs from Attic law it is generally to subject the slave more fully to the authority of his master and to create new obstacles in the way to freedom. It is true that the *Laws* outlines a "second-best" polity. But the contrast between the heavenly and the earthly city depends in part, as the *Politicus* affirms, on the presence or absence of absolute power in the organs of rule. From this consideration it is clear that the legitimacy of slavery would be even less subject to question in the heavenly than in the earthly city. Nor is there the slightest evidence for the assertion that slavery is absent in the "first-best" state described in the *Republic*.[4] It is true there is no mention of a slave class in addition to the three classes of citizens, but there are numerous references to slaves, and not one of them implies disapproval of slavery as an institution. One of the few laws in the *Republic* is the prohibition against owning Hellenic slaves;[5] but this, far from indicating that slavery is absent, suggests on the contrary that the presence of slaves of non-Hellenic origin is taken for granted. A Greek city without slaves was a thing almost unknown in Plato's time.[6]

---

[3] Ritter, *Kommentar*, p. 173; *Platon*, II, 604 ff.; Bisinger, *Der Agrarstaat in Platons Gesetzen*, p. 86.

[4] As Ritter contends (*Platon*, II, 604 ff.) and Adam (in his edition of the *Republic*, note on 469c). Adam's remark "where there is no οἰκία, as in Plato's state, there can be no οἰκέται," is singularly naïve. Barker (*Greek Political Theory*, p. 267n) who thinks it "dubious whether there is room for slavery of any sort" in the state described in the *Republic*, nevertheless replies to Adam that the οἰκία remains among the third class. One can also point out that the existence of public slaves, as at Athens, and of serfs, as at Sparta, was in no way related to the institution of the family. It is correct, I think, to assert that Plato did not contemplate a class of serfs in the ideal state; for serfdom is described (*Rep.* VIII, 547c) as coming into being when aristocracy degenerates into timocracy, and the warrior classes enslave the agricultural workers. This attitude toward serfdom is the same as that which is later expressed in the *Laws*. But we cannot infer that the possession of non-Hellenic personal slaves is intended to be excluded.

[5] *Rep.* V, 469c. Whoever believes that Plato would banish slavery entirely must follow the example of Wallon (I, 363) who concludes that Plato's ideal is the primitive state sketched in *Rep.* II, 369–373, not the τρυφῶσα πόλις of the main argument.

[6] Slave-holding is said to have been forbidden in Locris and Phocis (Timaeus, Fr. 67, Müller). In the remote parts of Greece the number of slaves was probably quite small.

If Plato had intended to picture a city without them, he would most certainly have felt impelled to say so explicitly and defend his proposal, as he defends his innovations regarding the education of women and the abolition of the family.

Those who have thought that Plato secretly disapproved of slavery have sometimes relied upon the extended discussion in Book VI, where, it is said, some hint is given of his real views.[7] We have already treated this passage at length and argued that Plato's reference to the distinction between master and slave as a "necessary" one is not to be taken as veiled disapproval, but rather as an assertion that the authority of the master over his slaves is one of the foundations of social order. The doubts and hesitations evident in the Athenian Stranger's remarks concern only particular forms of the institution and particular practices as regards slaves. Though he refers to "contradictory opinions" he does not mention the opinion that slavery is contrary to nature, a view we know was widely held at a date not much later than this and probably was well known at the time the *Laws* was written.[8] This doctrine, if Plato knew of it, evidently did not seem to him worth taking seriously.[9] There is no suggestion in the *Laws* nor in any other dialogue that he looked upon the relation of master and slave as wrong or

---

[7] See above, p. 34n, for the view of Apelt and Zimmern that this passage is a cautious assertion of the equality of all mankind. Ritter avoids the absurdity of making Plato an exponent of equality but nevertheless believes that he strongly disapproved of slavery. "Ich selbst bin der Meinung . . . dass Plato in der That jedes Verhältnis, das man ohne gröblichen Missbrauch des Wortes noch als 'Sklaverei' benennen dürfte, grundsätzlich verworfen und für verkehrt gehalten hat. Trotz dieser Überzeugung halte ich für zweifelhaft, ob hier [i.e. VI, 777b] diese Ansicht Platos zum consequenten Ausdruck gebracht ist, ob er sich nicht vielmehr hier wie meist in den *Gesetzen* der herrschenden Sitte und dem ihr dienenden Sprachgebrauch anbequemt hat" (*Kommentar*, p. 173). This view is also expressed and defended in Ritter's later work (*Platon*, II, 596–606). For criticism of Ritter's views, see below, note 11.

[8] The Sophist Alcidamas had declared in his *Messeniacus* that God has given all men freedom, that nature has made no man a slave (Blass, *Att. Bered.*, II, 350). Euripides put into the mouth of his dramatic personages expressions closely approaching this (*Ion* 854 ff.; Frags. 511 and 831 in Nauck's *Trag. Graec. Fragm.*). Such sentiments therefore must have been common even at the time the *Republic* was written. By the end of the century the Stoics were affirming the natural equality of all men. According to Zeno it was as great a crime to strike a slave as to strike a father (Diog. Laert. VII, 120; Cicero *De Fin.* IV, xxvii, 76). At the same time the unnaturalness of slavery was being expressed in a forthright manner by the dramatist Philemon (Frags. 22 and 95 in Kock's *Com. Att. Fragm.*). The Cynic Diogenes seems to have taught the same doctrine, which is sufficient to assure us of its familiarity to the citizens of Athens.

[9] Aristotle does mention it and in such a fashion as to show us that it was not Plato's view. For he specifically contrasts it with the doctrine that the power of the master is a kind of science (ἐπιστήμη) analogous to the rule of a king over his subjects. The latter view, as is evident from Aristotle's remarks, is Plato's. Cf. *Pol.* 1253b 14 ff.; and 1252a 7 ff.

unnatural. Plato criticizes, indeed, certain abuses connected with slavery, both in the *Laws* and elsewhere. He criticizes the great freedom that slaves enjoy in a democracy (*Rep.* VIII, 563b), and ridicules the ambitious freedman who, having just been emancipated, plans to marry his former master's daughter (*Rep.* VI, 495). He looks with aristocratic disdain upon the brutal master and remarks that the really cultured man will not demean himself by speaking harshly to his slaves (*Rep.* VIII, 549). But this is far from condemning the distinction between slave and free; it is rather to accept and emphasize it. There is such an agreement between the tone and temper of these remarks and the legislation of the *Laws* that it is somewhat naive, to say the least, to believe that Plato in the latter work is simply yielding to the force of reigning opinion.

The attempt to make Plato out to be an opponent of slavery finally breaks down when we note how well the distinction between slave and freeman set up in his law accords with his fundamental political principles. Both the *Republic* and the *Laws* insist that justice and equality demand the subordination of the inferior to the superior. To assign to all men an equal status, with equal rights and duties, is to act contrary to nature. There is, in any rightly organized society, a just and inevitable differentiation of status, and a corresponding differentiation of rights and duties. Thus the distinction between slave and master, like that between child and father, or citizen and public official, is grounded in necessary diversities of function in the social group and inevitable distinctions of quality among human beings. Since the slave nature is inferior to the free, the slave's δουλεία is a subjection to legitimate authority. This is the kind of justification that Plato might have given for admitting slavery into the *Laws;* in fact it is the apology that an eminent modern admirer has put forward.[10] But this line of thought overlooks certain considerations, considerations which of course are more obvious to us today than they were to Plato. If such a system of differing rights and duties is to be just, as well as necessary, then the right to exercise power and the duty of subordination must depend upon capacity or merit, not heredity, as Plato had himself recognized in the *Republic.* Furthermore, there must be a system of law declaring what the rights of the superior are, and who is qualified to exercise them, and providing adequate remedies for protecting the inferior party

---

[10] Ritter, pp. 175–176; cf. also p. 162.

against the unauthorized exercise of power. It is easy and natural to connect (as both Plato and his defenders have sometimes done) the moral antithesis between weakness or ignorance and rational self-control with the legal distinction between slave and freeman; just as it is easy to confuse obedience under law to legitimate authority with subjection without legal remedy to the power of a superior. When such legal remedies are lacking there is nothing to prevent the power of the superior from degenerating into brutal and arbitrary tyranny. In Plato's state the slave is in a real sense outside the law (*ἀκοινώνητος τῶν νόμων*) because he lacks the assurance that only law can give (and the law, alas! can only partially give it) that his δουλεία will be a subjection to legitimate authority and not merely to superior might.[11]

This criticism of Plato is all the more pertinent because he had himself, in a different connection, seen the fundamental point involved. Conceiving of ruling as a science, he first drew the implication that qualified rulers should enjoy absolute power, untrammeled by law. But he was led by sad experience to see that qualified rulers are rare and that law is the only safeguard of justice in human affairs. The primary application of this principle he saw clearly, viz. that political power should never be absolute, but should always be subject to legal restrictions. But the rule of masters over their slaves is also a form of δεσποτεία, and here also law is necessary as a safeguard of justice. Unfortunately Plato failed to make this application of his own principle.

---

[11] Ritter overlooks these elementary principles of legal justice in his cautious defense of the position Plato assigns the slaves in the *Laws*. It is true that the "true equality" (ἀληθεστάτη ἰσότης) Plato commends does lead, when logically carried out, to the δουλεία (in one sense of the word; see Appendix B) of the less gifted natures. But this δουλεία consists in obedience to legitimate authority and is to be sharply distinguished from the legal status of slavery, which alone is here in question. Thus it is misleading to compare the δουλεία in the *Laws* with the position of the third class in the *Republic*, for this class, however subordinate its function in the state, was still possessed of legal rights and legal capacity. One would have to think of them as lacking not only political power but also citizenship and civil rights before their condition would be analogous to that of the slaves in the *Laws*. When one keeps these distinctions in mind, one will hardly agree with Ritter that most men would prefer to be slaves rather than citizens in Plato's state, or that Plato's attitude is essentially in accord with the Christian recognition of the worth of all men.

APPENDIX

A. Δοῦλος AND οἰκέτης

It has been suggested that δοῦλος is the term used generally of a person in the servile status, while οἰκέτης is used when the slave's relation to his master is in mind (Klaar, in *Philol. Wochenschrift*, 1923, pp. 525–528). The distinction between the two terms would thus be analogous to that between *libertus* and *libertinus* in Roman law. The author of this interesting suggestion finds it confirmed by Plato's use of the two terms, and more specifically by *Laws* VI, 776b–778a. This passage concerns the proper treatment of slaves by their masters (see above, p. 33) and in such a context, if Klaar's theory is correct, we should expect to find οἰκέτης predominating; but δοῦλος appears fully as often. What is more, the two terms appear to be interchangeable. Thus masters are enjoined to avoid *hybris* toward οἰκέται and unholiness toward δοῦλοι; they are to punish δοῦλοι justly and address οἰκέται always in a tone of command; they are not to allow the οἰκέται to become arrogant, for when δοῦλοι are thus spoiled their lot is harder to bear, etc. If there is any such distinction between the terms as Klaar affirms, Plato seems studiously to avoid it. There are other places in the *Laws* where one would particularly expect to find οἰκέτης, according to this theory: e.g., the provisions covering the killing of a master by his own slave (IX, 868b), the killing of a slave by his own master (IX, 868a), and sexual relations between a master and his slave or a mistress and her slave (XI, 930d). But in all these cases δοῦλος appears. On the other hand we find οἱ τῆς πόλεως οἰκέται (VII, 794b)—a very odd expression if οἰκέτης carried a reference to the master, since the public slaves had no masters, in the legal sense of the word. And if Klaar's theory is correct, how are we to explain Antiphon V, 48? The law allows the master, Antiphon says, to prosecute for his slave (ἐπεξελθεῖν ὑπὲρ τοῦ δούλου, where we should certainly expect οἰκέτου).

It has sometimes been asserted that in the law of Gortyn δῶλος denoted the domestic or personal slave, οἰκεύς the serf (Kohler-Ziebarth, p. 50; Bücheler-Zitelmann, pp. 63 ff., recognize that δῶλος is also used in the wider and more general sense). But further analysis of the text seems to have shown this belief to be erroneous (Busolt, p. 286n). Like their Attic equivalents, these terms seem to be used without any material distinction in meaning.

B. The Various Meanings of δουλεία in Plato

Plato uses the word δουλεία and its cognates not merely to denote the social-legal status ordinarily called slavery, but also in at least three other senses. These other meanings are always floating about threatening to confuse Plato's commentators, if in fact they did not sometimes deceive Plato himself.

1. Sometimes it means the absence of political rights or of political independence. Thus the final stage of political degeneracy described in the *Republic*, when the citizens are helpless beneath the power of a tyrant, is characterized as a state of the most extreme and savage slavery (VIII,

564a, 569c, 575d, 576a). And in the *Laws* the subjects of absolute monarchies are called slaves (VI, 756e; IV, 713a).[1] But of course the persons living under a Greek tyrant or an oriental monarch were not δοῦλοι in the sense of being chattels of their political superior. The tyrant might sometimes sell some of his subjects into slavery, if his power was great enough, but the distinction between slaves and freemen persisted within the body of his subjects, no matter how tyrannical his government. The same is true of the oriental despotisms; personal slavery might on occasion be a consequence of political despotism, but it was not identical with it. Again, Plato sometimes speaks of the enslaving of one state by another, as when the Persians enslaved the Greek cities of Asia Minor (*Menex.* 239d, 244e ff.; cf. *Polit.* 308a, *Rep.* I, 351b). What is meant is that these cities lost their political independence (the ἐλευθερία καὶ αὐτονομία which appears so often in the inscriptions; e.g. *Syll.* Nos. 147, 148, 322, 344, 374, 409), not that all their inhabitants were reduced to chattel slavery. The latter might on occasion follow upon the loss of political independence, but it was legally and politically something distinct and worse.

2. Again it denotes certain inferior or servile traits of character, such as preoccupation with trifles (*Symp.* 210d), or absorption in practical affairs to the neglect of theoretical inquiries (*Theaet.* 173a), or inability to control desire and passion (*Crito* 52c, *Rep.* IX, 577cd), or incapacity of apprehending a rational principle (Laws IV, 720b)—in short anything incompatible with the ideal of the free man (ὁ ἐλεύθερος) in the moral (not the legal) sense of the word. Such traits are regarded as especially characteristic of the slave, in the legal sense of the term, but they are often attributed, as the above passages show, to persons who are freemen before the law.

3. Lastly, it sometimes denotes the status and function of any subordinate member of a whole. Thus Plato frequently refers to the lower part or parts of the soul as in bondage to (δουλεύοντα) the higher (*Phaedo* 79e; *Rep.* IV, 444b; IX, 577d; *Laws* V, 726). In the *Philebus* τὸ δουλεῦον denotes any subordinate principle or characteristic (27a; 58b; cf. *Ep. VIII*, 355b). But the term may be applied to any person who obeys or serves, as a child obeying his parents or tutors (*Lysis* 208e), or a citizen obeying the state's officers or the state's laws (*Apol.* 37c; *Rep.* VIII, 563d, 569b). This use of the term occurs with peculiar frequency in the *Laws* (III, 698bc, 699c, 701b; IV, 715d; VI, 762e; IX, 856b; X, 890a; cf. also *Ep. VIII*, 354c–e). The Athenian Stranger is never weary of preaching "slavery to the laws" (δουλεύειν τοῖς νόμοις) as the saving principle of all political order. "In ancient times," he says, "the people was not as now the master, but rather the willing servant of the laws" (ἑκὼν ἐδούλευε τοῖς νόμοις, III, 700a). In this use of the word δουλεία has a positive value, for the slavery of the naturally inferior to the naturally superior is a subjection to legitimate authority and is right and satisfying. We are even told that slavery in this sense is more to be extolled than the art of ruling; for no one can ever be a praiseworthy master who has not been a slave (VI, 762e).

---

[1] Δουλεία and ἐλευθερία are often regarded as opposite extremes of political disorder. See *Laws* III, 694a, 698a; *Ep.* VIII, 354e.

INDEX OF PASSAGES IN PLATO

(The numbers in italics refer to pages in this book.)

GENERAL INDEX

HISTORY OF IDEAS
IN
ANCIENT GREECE

An Arno Press Collection

Albertelli, Pilo. **Gli Eleati**: Testimonianze E Frammenti. 1939

Allman, George Johnston. **Greek Geometry From Thales To Euclid**. 1889

Apelt, Otto. **Platonische Aufsätze**. 1912

Aristotle. **Aristotle De Anima**. With Translation, Introduction and Notes by R[obert] D[rew] Hicks. 1907

Aristotle. **Aristotle's Psychology**. With Introduction and Notes by Edwin Wallace. 1882

Aristotle. **The Politics of Aristotle**. A Revised Text With Introduction, Analysis and Commentary by Franz Susemihl and R[obert] D[rew] Hicks. 1894. Books I-V

Arnim, Hans [Friedrich August von]. **Platos Jugenddialoge Und Die Entstehungszeit Des Phaidros**. 1914

Arpe, Curt. **Das τί ἦν εἶναι Bei Aristoteles** and Hambruch, Ernst, **Logische Regeln Der Platonischen Schule In Der Aristotelischen Topik**. 1938/1904. Two vols. in one

Beauchet, Ludovic. **Histoire Du Droit Privé De La République Athénienne**. 1897. Four vols.

Boeckh, Augustus. **The Public Economy of Athens**. 1842

Daremberg, Ch[arles]. **La Médecine**: Histoire Et Doctrines. 1865

Dareste, Rodolphe [de la Chavanne]. **La Science Du Droit En Grèce**: Platon, Aristote, Théophraste. 1893

Derenne, Eudore. **Les Procès D'Impiété Intentés Aux Philosophes A Athènes Au Vme Et Au IVme Siècles Avant J. C.** 1930

Diès, A[uguste]. **Autour De Platon**: Essais De Critique Et D'Histoire. 1927

Dittmar, Heinrich. **Aischines Von Sphettos**: Studien Zur Literaturgeschichte Der Sokratiker. 1912

Dugas, L[udovic]. **L'Amitié Antique D'Après Les Moeurs Populaires Et Les Théories Des Philosophes**. 1894

Fredrich, Carl. **Hippokratische Untersuchungen**. 1899

Freeman, Kathleen. **The Work And Life Of Solon**, With A Translation Of His Poems. 1926

Frisch, Hartvig. **The Constitution Of The Athenians**. 1942

Frisch, Hartvig. **Might And Right In Antiquity**. "Dike" I: From Homer To The Persian Wars. 1949

Frutiger, Perceval. **Les Mythes De Platon**: Étude Philosophique Et Littéraire. 1930

Heidel, William Arthur. **The Frame Of The Ancient Greek Maps**. 1937

Heidel, W[illiam] A[rthur]. **Plato's Euthyphro,** With Introduction and Notes and **Pseudo-Platonica.** [1902]/1896. Two vols. in one

Hermann, Karl Fr[iedrich]. **Geschichte Und System Der Platonischen Philosophie.** 1839. Part One all published

Hirzel, Rudolf. **Die Person:** Begriff Und Name Derselben Im Altertum and Uxkull-Gyllenband, Woldemar Graf, **Griechische Kultur-Entstehungslehren.** 1914/1924. Two vols. in one

Kleingünther, Adolf. ΠΡΩΤΟΣ ΕΥΡΕΤΗΣ: Untersuchungen Zur Geschichte Einer Fragestellung. 1933

Krohn, A[ugust A.] **Der Platonische Staat.** 1876

Mahaffy, J. P. **Greek Life And Thought From The Age Of Alexander To The Roman Conquest.** 1887

Martin, Th[omas] Henri. **Études Sur Le Timée De Platon.** 1841. Two vols. in one

Martin, Th[omas] H[enri]. **Mémoire Sur Les Hypothèses Astronomiques.** 1879/1881. Three parts in one

Milhaud, Gaston. **Les Philosophes-Géomètres De La Grèce.** 1900

Morrow, Glenn R. **Plato's Law Of Slavery In Its Relation To Greek Law.** 1939

Plato. **The Hippias Major Attributed To Plato.** With Introductory Essay and Commentary by Dorothy Tarrant. 1928

Plato. **The Laws Of Plato.** The Text Edited With Introduction and Notes by E. B. England. 1921. Two vols.

Saunders, Trevor J. **Bibliography On Plato's Laws, 1920-1970:** With Additional Citations Through May, 1975. 1975

Plato. **The Platonic Epistles.** Translated With Introduction and Notes by J. Harward. 1932

Raeder, Hans. **Platons Philosophische Entwickelung.** 1905

Ritter, Constantin. **Neue Untersuchungen Über Platon.** 1910

Ritter, Constantin. **Platon:** Sein Leben, Seine Schriften, Seine Lehre. 1910/1923. Two vols.

Sachs, Eva. **Die Fünf Platonischen Körper.** 1917

Schwartz, Eduard. **Ethik Der Griechen.** 1951

Shute, Richard. **On The History Of The Process By Which The Aristotelian Writings Arrived At Their Present Form.** 1888

Snell, Bruno. **Die Ausdrücke Für Den Begriff Des Wissens In Der Vorplatonischen Philosophie.** 1924

Tannery, Paul. **La Géométrie Grecque.** 1887

Tannery, Paul. **Recherches Sur L'Histoire De L'Astronomie Ancienne.** 1893

Taylor, A. E. **Philosophical Studies.** 1934

Wallace, Edwin, compiler. **Outlines Of The Philosophy Of Aristotle.** 1894

Zeller, Eduard. **Platonische Studien.** 1839

Zeno And The Discovery Of Incommensurables In Greek Mathematics. 1975